The GLOBAL BAKERY

Amazing Cakes from the World's Kitchens

The Global Bakery: Amazing Cakes from the World's Kitchens

Published in the UK in 2014 by New Internationalist Publications Ltd
The Old Music Hall
106-108 Cowley Road
Oxford OX4 1JE, UK
newint.org

About the author
Anna Weston has been an enthusiastic cake baker for many years. She takes great pleasure in adapting recipes to create new flavors and then trying out the results on her friends and colleagues at New Internationalist. She is passionate about communicating the message that cake baking is not just for the experts and that all over the world delicious cakes have always been produced in domestic kitchens with rudimentary equipment and ingredients.

Design: Andrew Kokotka
Food photography: Graham Alder/MM Studios

Printed by 1010 Printing International Ltd, who hold environmental accreditation ISO 14001.

British Library Cataloguing-in-Publication Data
A catalogue record for this book is available from the British Library.

Library of Congress Cataloging-in-Publication Data
A catalog record for this book is available from the Library of Congress.

Hardback ISBN 978-1-78026-216-1
Paperback ISBN 978-1-78026-125-6
ebook ISBN 978-1-78026-189-8

The GLOBAL BAKERY

Amazing Cakes from the World's Kitchens

Anna Weston

New Internationalist

The Cakes

Sub-Saharan Africa

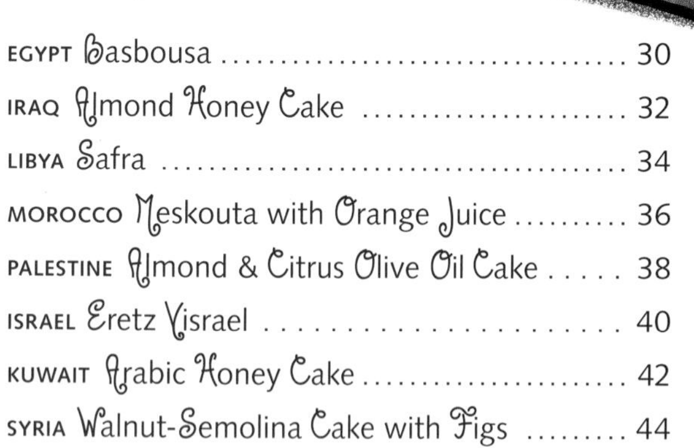

Middle East & North Africa

Europe

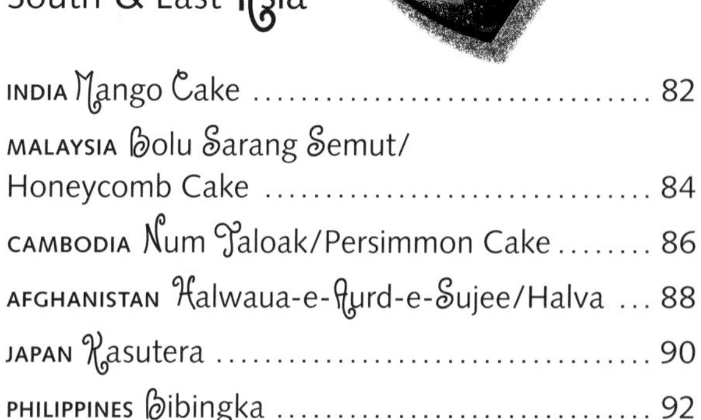

South & East Asia

Caribbean & North America

Oceania & Pacific

Latin America

Eastern Europe & Central Asia

HAPPY BAKING!

Introduction

For as long as I can remember I have taken pleasure in baking, from helping my mother make the cakes that kept us going when we came in hungry from school right through to the various birthday cake challenges set by my children over the years, which usually tested my icing skills above all. I see making a cake at home for family and friends as a gesture of love and affection, while the unmistakable aroma of baking in the house simply makes me happy. However, I had reached the stage where I was becoming a little bored with baking traditional cakes using the tried and tested methods and recipes that I had used from childhood. So, given that I have worked as office manager at New Internationalist for 10 years now, dealing with people from all over the world on an everyday basis, I started to wonder about the wider world of baking. Working on the premise that every culture must have a cake, and armed with a list of all the countries in the world, I started researching the wonders of baking in corners of the globe that I am never likely to visit in the flesh. I soon discovered an amazing richness of cakes from every corner of the globe and found myself investigating cakes and delicacies that are well beyond the scope of most other books about baking – let alone my mother's fund of knowledge.

Cakes used to be a luxury items, baked when times were good and ingredients plentiful. Of course, they also marked times of celebration and religious or special occasions, but there was usually a purpose to their production. They were often the result of a good harvest or a way of using up a glut of fruit at certain times of the year. At other times they might even be made from the leftovers of the main course, sweetened and baked up again in a new form because food was too precious to be wasted. Today, baking is seen as a creative hobby rather than a weekly task, and we give little thought to the origins of the recipes we use, but many of the cakes featured here were once only possible at certain times of the year. The

EFTHYMIA ANASTASIOU

Italian cake Castagnaccio, for instance, which you can find on page 60, was traditionally made in autumn during the chestnut season: it is made with chestnut flour, sweetened with raisins and flavored with rosemary. Many of the cakes in the book use ingredients that are grown in the country of origin and only baked when a certain fruit is in season. We have divided the book by region and you will inevitably find the same ingredients repeated within the recipes in those regional sections – but I can assure you that the baked results taste very different.

While writing the book I have learned new methods of preparation and have had to forget many of the traditional rules of baking that I previously took for granted. Western recipes for cakes and sponges tend to specify, for example, that the oven door should not be opened nor the cake removed until it is fully baked, whereas some of the recipes in the book actively encourage it. Take Arab Honey Cake from Kuwait (page 42): this is put in the oven while the topping is made, removed so that the topping can be added, and then put back in the oven to finish baking – but what a fantastic result! Mind you, I would urge you to take note of the warning about the reaction to expect when adding baking soda to simmering milk for the Jugu Cake from East Africa (page 16), as it does froth in the most alarming way. But in this case, as in all the others, if you follow the step-by-step instructions and hold your nerve, things will work out fine.

You can rest assured that I have baked all the cakes in my kitchen at home more than once – first to make sure that the recipe is absolutely right, and ultimately so that we could photograph the results for the book. The recipes have also been tested for taste by my colleagues in the New Internationalist office who, with no regard for their personal safety, ate their way through all 64 cakes – although not all at once!

In East Oxford we are fortunate enough to be surrounded by a rich diversity of foodstuffs aimed at the many different immigrant communities. With a little searching in Asian, East European or African shops, I tracked down the spices, flours and fruits I needed. It was intriguing to use ingredients that I had never even heard of before I started researching these recipes. For example, I had never used jaggery or peen tong, both of which are solid sugars that are sold in blocks. The blocks are either broken up or grated, then dissolved in water, forming a liquid that can be added to dry ingredients. I have since found out that, historically, sugar used to be bought in cones even in the West, and had to be broken up in households before modern refining methods gave us the huge choice that is now before us. Don't be disheartened, however, if you live in an area that is not so richly endowed with multicultural stores – I have generally suggested alternatives for the more obscure ingredients that will still produce a delicious cake.

Some of the cakes here are made with semolina, rice or corn flours, which makes them suitable for cake lovers with gluten intolerance, and the book also contains cakes made with finely ground nuts – as with Tarta de Santiago (page 76), which is baked using ground almonds instead of flour. There are also cakes here that will suit people with a dairy intolerance, made with oil rather than butter. There were just one or two ingredients that were not greeted with enthusiasm by all comers – most notably, the sugared and colored sweet potato in the cake from Taiwan (page 94) was met with some suspicion by my team of cake tasters. But the joy of this book is that it takes both the cook and the tasters out of their comfort zones. Incidentally, even if you also do not fancy the filling of that particular Taiwanese recipe, do bake the sponge anyway using jam or fruit preserve inside instead of the sweet potato, as it makes a great Swiss roll.

There are some recipes in the book for readers who are new to baking, while others may appeal more to experienced cake bakers. Some of them are really quick and easy and would be great for introducing children to baking (such as the Welsh Barabrith on page 78). Others are more challenging and involve several stages before you can assemble the finished item and wow your friends and family with your achievement (the Cuban Opera Cake on page 120 will certainly do that). But in all cases I have broken the instructions down into easy steps so that, even when you are entering uncharted territory, if you work through the stages methodically all will become clear. I would advise you to read the recipes through first and to weigh all the ingredients before starting so that you don't miss anything out. I have flagged up possible pitfalls and will freely admit to having made some errors myself, usually when trying to take shortcuts – when preparing the Maple Syrup Cake (page 108), for instance, I covered myself, the kitchen and the dog in powdered sugar just because I decided to use an electric whisk to make the icing!

Welcome to the wonders of the Global Bakery. Investigating it has been a fantastic adventure for me and I hope it will be just as much of a delight for you.

Anna Weston

Glossary

Bundt pan
A bundt pan is round, with a hole or chimney in the middle. The design allows more of the mixture to touch the surface of the pan than in a traditional round cake pan, resulting in faster and more even heat distribution during baking. The pans are available in aluminium and silicone and many have decorative fluting. The hole in the middle of the finished cake can be filled with fruit and cream. Plain versions are also known as tube pans.

Spring-form pan
A spring-form pan is useful when baking delicate cakes and cheesecakes. It consists of a round base and an interlocking band that forms the sides when closed with the flick of spring latch. When the cake is cooled, the side can be released so that the cake does not have to tipped upside down to get it out. Spring-form pans are not watertight around the base so they have to be lined with foil to prevent runny batter from leaking out.

Silicone pans
Silicone pans have many advantages over traditional aluminium and glass pans. They require little or no greasing as they are non-stick. They are easy to clean and store as they can be rolled or flattened but will spring back into shape. They are rust-proof, can be used in microwaves and freezers and are oven safe up to 240°C/465°F. However, they are not as stable as traditional pans and should be put into the oven on a baking tray for safe and easy removal while the cake is hot.

Loose-bottomed cake pan
A loose-bottomed cake pan consists of a round base and solid band for the side. The base is held firmly within the band. It is suitable for making cheesecakes and delicate cakes made with a runny batter, although it may still be advisable to line the pan with foil or paper to be absolutely sure. The cake is removed by simply pushing the base up or by standing the pan on a tin can so that the sides just fall away, leaving the cake intact.

Parchment/greaseproof paper
Parchment/greaseproof paper is resistant to oil and grease. It is used in baking to line cake pans to prevent leakage and to ensure that the cake does not stick. It is most effective when the cake pan is greased or oiled, lined with the greaseproof paper and then greased or oiled again. It is also known as cook's paper, baking paper and butter paper.

Swiss roll/Jelly roll/Sponge roll pan
This is an oblong, low-sided pan that is used to bake a fat-free sponge for rolling and filling with jam and/or cream. The standard dimensions are 9 x 13 inches (23 x 33 cm) and 3/4 inch (1.9 cm) deep. It is advisable to line even non-stick versions with parchment paper to ensure that the sponge does not stick.

CAKE LIST

Sub-Saharan Africa

RECIPES FROM...

West Africa

Mali

Côte d'Ivoire

Ghana

East Africa

Zimbabwe

South Africa

CÔTE D'IVOIRE

Gâteau Moelleux à l'Ananas et à la Noix de Coco

Soft Cake with Pineapple and Coconut

prep 20 mins/bake 20 mins

Some ingredients are just made for each other and that is the case with pineapple and coconut. In this cake, the flavors of each of them remain distinct despite the smooth texture. It would work just as well as a dessert served warm with crème fraîche or cream.

½ cup / 100 g butter, melted
½ cup / 90 g grated fresh coconut
⅔ cup / 130 g caster sugar
3 eggs, beaten
1½ cups / 195 g all-purpose/plain flour
1 tsp baking powder
pinch of salt
1½ cups / 300 g chopped fresh pineapple pieces with juice

Grease and flour an 8-inch/20-cm spring-form cake pan.
Heat the oven to 375°F/190°C/Gas Mark 5.

1. In a large bowl, combine the melted butter and grated coconut.
2. Add the sugar and beaten eggs and mix well.
3. Sift the flour, baking powder and salt into the mixture.
4. Fold in the pineapple pieces and juice.
5. Transfer the mixture to the prepared cake pan and bake for 20 minutes or until a skewer inserted in the middle comes out clean and the top is golden brown.
6. Remove the cake from the oven and let it cool for 10 minutes before releasing the pan.

EAST AFRICA

Jugu Cake

Peanut Cake

prep 20 mins/bake 25 mins

The word *Jugu* means peanut in Kiswahili. This cake from East Africa is similar to biscotti in flavor but is chewier and denser and is also a perfect accompaniment for coffee. Make sure you use a large bowl for combining all the ingredients before forming the cake dough and do look out when you add the baking soda to the milk – it froths in quite an alarming way! This recipe makes a lot of cake and so is great for donating to cake stalls and fundraising events.

3 cups / 400 g roasted unsalted peanuts for grinding
3 tbsp roughly chopped roasted unsalted peanuts
5 cups / 650 g all-purpose/plain flour
2 cups / 400 g caster sugar
2 tsp baking powder
3 eggs – separate one egg yolk and keep it in a separate bowl
½ cup / 90 g butter
1 tsp baking soda
1 cup / 240 ml whole milk

Heat the oven to 355°F/180°C/Gas Mark 4.

1. Grind the peanuts until they resemble a mealy but not fine texture.
2. Combine the ground peanuts, flour, white sugar and baking powder in a large mixing bowl and make a well in the middle of the mixture.
3. Melt the butter and pour it into the well.
4. Beat the eggs (three whites and two yolks) and add to the ingredients.
5. Warm the milk in a pan, until it is simmering.
6. Add the baking soda to the milk and pour into the mixture while it is frothing.
7. With your hands, and working quickly, combine the ingredients until the mixture forms a soft dough.
8. Tip the dough onto a lightly floured work surface, form into a large sausage shape and divide into five equal portions.
9. Roll each piece into a roll about 12 inches / 30 cm in length, and place onto a greased baking sheet leaving a slight gap between each roll. You might want to move the baking sheet close to where you are working to prevent tearing when carrying back and forth.
10. Beat the remaining egg yolk, brush it onto the rolls and then sprinkle them with the roughly chopped peanuts.
11. Bake for 30 minutes or until golden brown and a skewer inserted in the rolls comes out clean.
12. Allow the rolls to cool before cutting or tearing them apart.

SOUTH AFRICA

Bienenstich

Bee Sting Cake

prep 40 mins/bake 35-45 mins

There are several stories behind the name of this cake but the one I am choosing to believe is that the baker who invented it was stung by a bee as it was put on display! The toffee and almond topping provides a contrast to the smooth filling. Take your time when making the vanilla custard – it's worth the effort to make your own and it tastes wonderful. There is ample filling to fill three layers but I prefer the decadence of an over-filled cake!

2 cups / 260 g all-purpose/plain flour
3 tsp baking powder
½ tsp salt
½ cup / 125 g butter
½ cup / 100 g caster sugar
1 tsp vanilla extract
2 eggs
½ cup / 120 ml milk

Topping
¼ cup / 60 g butter
4 tbsp / 60 g caster sugar
½ cup / 100 g sliced almonds
1 tbsp milk

Filling
1 cup / 240 ml milk
1 cup / 240 ml cream
2 egg yolks
4 tbsp / 60 g caster sugar
3½ tbsp corn starch/cornflour
1 tsp vanilla extract
2 tbsp / 30 g butter

Heat the oven to 355°F/180°C/Gas Mark 4.
Grease and flour a 9-inch/23-cm spring-form cake pan.

1. Sift flour, baking powder and salt into a bowl and set aside.
2. Cream the butter and sugar until light and fluffy. Add the vanilla extract.
3. Add the eggs one at a time, beating well after each addition.
4. Add the sifted dry ingredients, alternating with the milk, until the mixture is smooth and creamy.
5. Pour the mixture into the prepared pan and set aside. Prepare the topping before the cake goes into the oven.
6. To make the topping, combine all the ingredients in a small saucepan and stir over a medium heat until the sugar has dissolved. Pour the mixture over the cake batter, spreading it evenly.
7. Bake the cake for 35-45 minutes, or until a skewer inserted in the middle comes out clean.
8. While cake is in the oven, make the custard filling.
9. Beat together the corn starch/cornflour, sugar, egg yolks and vanilla extract until the mixture is light and creamy.

10 In a small saucepan, heat the milk and cream until just simmering.

11 Slowly, and in a thin stream, add the hot milk to the cream mixture, whisking all the while. Stir well.

12 Transfer the mixture back into the saucepan and cook over a low-to-medium heat. Keep stirring and whisking until the mixture thickens well. Do not be tempted to increase the heat as the custard will separate and/or burn.

13 Stir in the butter, remove from the heat, and allow the filling to cool.

14 When the cake comes out of the oven, allow it to cool in the pan for 15 minutes, then release it.

15 When the cake has thoroughly cooled, cut it into two layers using a long serrated knife. Spread all the custard on the bottom layer, then place the other layer, with its crunchy topping, on top.

MALI

Gâteau de Semoule aux Agrumes

Wheat free

Semolina and Citrus Cake

prep 20 mins/bake 35 mins

Although this cake has the consistency of a firm blancmange, it can be sliced and holds its shape well. The smooth, creamy texture and citrus 'tang' give it a special quality and it is all the better for not being too sweet.

1 unwaxed orange or lemon
2 cups / 480 ml whole milk
1 cup / 180 g fine semolina flour
1 cup / 200 g caster sugar
pinch of salt
4 eggs
2 tsp honey
Clear honey to drizzle

Heat the oven to 355°F/180°C/Gas Mark 4.

Grease an 8-inch/20-cm spring-form cake pan and line it with parchment paper.

1. Finely grate the zest from the orange or lemon and set aside then squeeze the juice from the orange or lemon.
2. Pour the milk into a pan and remove it from the heat just as it boils.
3. Pour the hot milk over the semolina in a heat-proof bowl, stirring constantly until smooth. If lumps form, give the mixture a quick beating with a hand-held mixer.
4. Scrape the mixture back into the saucepan and cook it gently over a low heat, stirring constantly, until the mixture thickens.
5. Remove the mixture from the heat and stir in the sugar, orange/lemon zest and juice of the orange/lemon along with a pinch of salt.
6. Add the eggs, one at a time, beating the mixture well to combine.
7. Add the two teaspoons of honey.
8. Pour the mixture into the cake pan and bake for 35 minutes, or until the top is golden brown and a skewer inserted in the middle comes out clean.
9. Remove the cake from the oven and allow it to cool completely in the pan before turning it out.
10. Refrigerate the cake for at least three hours before serving.
11. To serve, slice the cake into wedges and then drizzle them with honey.

WEST AFRICA

Lime Cake

prep 10 mins/bake 25 mins

Children will enjoy making and decorating this easy cake, which both looks and tastes very fresh. The glacé icing has a definite zing as it is made with lime juice. If you use fresh lime slices for decoration, remember to blot them for a few minutes first to soak up the excess juice.

1 cup / 200 g caster sugar
2½ tbsp / 35 g butter
2 eggs, beaten
1 lime, juice of
1½ cups / 195 g all-purpose/plain flour
2 tsp baking powder

Icing
1 cup / 135 g confectioner's/icing sugar
1 lime, juice of
Green food coloring

Grease and flour an 8-inch/20-cm square cake pan. Heat the oven to 355°F/180°C/Gas Mark 4.

1. Cream the sugar and butter until light and fluffy.
2. Add the beaten eggs and the lime juice and beat until thoroughly combined.
3. Add the flour and baking powder and fold into the batter until combined.
4. Pour the mixture into the cake pan and bake for 25 minutes, or until a skewer inserted in the middle comes out clean.
5. Allow the cake to cool in the pan for 10 minutes, then remove to a cake rack until it has completely cooled.
6. In a medium-sized bowl, sieve the confectioner's/icing sugar, then add the lime juice a little at a time until a glossy icing with a spreading consistency is achieved.
7. Add a couple of drops of green food coloring and stir well until the color is even. Spread the icing over the top of the cold cake. Decorate as desired.

GHANA

Banana and Peanut Cake

prep 15 mins/bake 30 mins

This is a good tea-time cake. It keeps for several days in an airtight container and the flavors seem to improve the longer it is kept. The mixture of cinnamon and confectioner's/icing sugar for the topping adds a spicy element, though be aware that when you add the sugar to the warm cake it will sink in and seem to disappear.

3 cups / 390 g all-purpose/plain flour
⅓ cup / 45 g cake/self-raising flour
2 tsp baking powder
1 tsp salt
½ tsp baking soda
¾ cup / 150 g butter
1 cup / 200 g caster sugar
2 eggs, lightly beaten
4 mashed bananas
1 cup / 100g coarsely chopped peanuts
¼ cup / 40 g coarsely chopped peanuts for decoration

Topping

½ cup / 70 g confectioner's/icing sugar
1 tsp cinnamon

Grease a 9-inch/23-cm x 5-inch/13-cm loaf pan. Heat the oven to 340°F/170°C/Gas Mark 3.

1. Sift the flours, baking powder, salt and baking soda into a bowl. Set aside.
2. In a large bowl, cream together the butter and sugar, then beat in the eggs, mixing well after each addition.
3. Mix the mashed banana with the larger amount of chopped peanuts.
4. Gradually fold the dry ingredients into the creamed mixture, alternating with the mix of mashed bananas and peanuts.
5. Mix thoroughly and pour into the prepared cake pan. Sprinkle with the remaining chopped peanuts.
6. The cake is ready when it is golden brown or when a skewer inserted in the middle of the cake comes out clean.
7. Combine the cinnamon and icing sugar and dust the mixture over the cake as soon as it comes out of the oven. Allow the cake to cool in the pan before removing it.

ZIMBABWE

Cornmeal Cake

Gluten free

prep 20 mins/bake 45 mins

With its bright yellow color and bubbled surface, this cake looks great on a plate. The unusual method results in a soft but firm cake with a slightly grainy texture. It tastes good hot or cold.

4¼ cups / 1 litre milk
2 eggs, beaten
¼ cup / 50 g butter, melted
½ cup / 100 g caster sugar
1 cup / 150 g medium cornmeal
1 tsp vanilla extract
½ cup / 120 ml sour cream

Grease an 8-inch/20-cm diameter spring-form cake pan. Line the pan with baking parchment and grease again.

Heat the oven to 340°F/170°C/Gas Mark 3.

1. Pour the milk into a saucepan and heat until it is just boiling. Take it off the heat then set it aside to cool for 10 minutes.
2. Whisk the beaten eggs, butter and sugar into the warm milk. Gently bring the mixture to a boil then take it off the heat again and add the cornmeal in a steady stream, stirring constantly to prevent lumps (have a hand-held whisk at the ready to give the mixture a good beating should lumps start to form).
3. Return to a low heat and continue cooking gently until the mixture has thickened, stirring all the while to prevent sticking.
4. Add the vanilla extract, stir it in well and then take the saucepan off the heat.
5. Pour the melted butter into the cake pan. Swirl it so that it completely coats the pan then pour in the thickened cornmeal mixture.
6. Bake the mixture for about 30 minutes, or until the cake is cooked through, golden and a skewer inserted in the middle comes out clean.
7. Remove the cake from the oven and pour the sour cream over it. Return to the oven and continue baking for 15 minutes, or until the top is bubbly and lightly browned. You may need to turn the cake while it is browning to give it an even color.
8. Allow the cake to cool for 10 minutes then remove it from the pan. Serve it while still warm or leave it to cool completely.

CAKE LIST

Middle East & North Africa

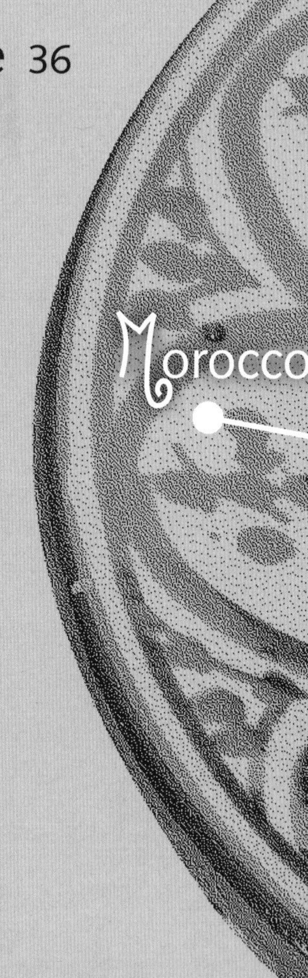

RECIPES FROM...

EGYPT

Basbousa

Wheat free

prep 20 mins/bake 25 mins

When I brought this into the office to try out on my poor unsuspecting colleagues, someone commented that it made her day seem much brighter! You will need to make the syrup first, as it is poured over the cake as soon as it comes out of the oven. The syrup could also be flavored by adding two tablespoons of rose water to the sugar and water, though, if you do this, don't forget to reduce the water by two tablespoons. Either way, Basbousa is simple to make and delicious to eat.

3 cups / 540 g semolina flour
1 cup / 130 g all-purpose/plain flour
1 cup / 200 g caster sugar
1½ tsp baking powder
1 cup / 240 ml vegetable oil
1 cup / 240 ml milk

Syrup
1½ cups / 300 g caster sugar
1 cup / 240 ml water
1 lemon, juice and peel
3 tsp honey

Heat the oven to 355°F/180°C/Gas Mark 4. Grease a 10-inch/25.5-cm x 16-inch/40-cm shallow baking pan.

Syrup

1. Peel the lemon with a potato peeler to make flat strips of peel.
2. Juice the lemon.
3. Put the lemon juice, sugar and water in a small pan and bring to boiling point.
4. Add the rind of the lemon and continue boiling until the lemon rind is hard and the mixture is a runny syrup consistency.
5. Add the honey and stir until combined. Remove from the heat and set aside.

Cake

1. In a bowl, mix together the semolina flour, flour, sugar and baking powder.
2. Add the oil and mix until the ingredients are thoroughly combined.
3. Add the milk and mix until smooth.
4. Using a large spoon, drop spoonfuls of the mixture onto the greased pan then, using the palm of your hand dipped in milk, level the mixture in the tray.
5. Cut the mixture into squares or diamond shapes and place an almond in the middle of each portion.
6. Bake for 25 minutes or until golden brown.
7. Pour the syrup over the cake immediately after removing it from the oven.
8. Allow the cake to cool in the pan.

IRAQ

Almond Honey Cake Wheat free/Gluten free

prep 15 mins/bake 30 mins

Honey and almonds are such a good combination and this cake has plenty of both. This recipe for honey cake uses ground almonds rather than flour as its base and is therefore perfect to serve anyone with a gluten allergy. It is also very moist. The trick of sprinkling the baking powder over the mixture to stop the cake sinking certainly works! Surprisingly, the cake is not too sweet so the drizzle of honey to finish it off does not take it over the top.

- 1¾ cups / 185 g ground almonds
- 4 eggs, separated
- ¾ cup / 180 ml clear honey, plus 2 tbsp
- 1 tsp vanilla
- ½ tsp baking powder
- Pinch of salt

Butter a 9-inch/23-cm cake pan.
Heat the oven to 355°F/180°C/Gas Mark 4.

1. Combine the ground almonds, egg yolks, honey, salt and vanilla, mixing well until thoroughly incorporated. Set aside.
2. In a separate bowl, whip the egg whites until foamy but not stiff or forming peaks.
3. Gently fold the egg whites into the almond mixture and stir carefully.
4. Sprinkle the baking powder over the mixture and combine gently to incorporate thoroughly. Adding the baking powder at this stage will ensure that the cake is not dense and lessens the risk of the middle sinking.
5. Pour the batter into the cake pan. Gently tap the pan on a hard surface to knock out air bubbles in the batter.
6. Bake for approximately 30 minutes or until golden brown and a skewer inserted in the middle comes out clean.
7. Allow to cool. Serve with honey drizzled over the top.

LIBYA

Safra

Wheat free/Vegan

Semolina and Date Cake

prep 25 mins/bake 35-40 mins

The moist and spicy date filling and topping is the highlight of this sandwich cake. It is worth waiting for the syrup to completely soak through as it allows the flavor of the lemon and spices to develop. For that reason this is a good cake to bake in the morning to enjoy later in the day.

- 5 cups / 900 g semolina (fine or medium)
- 2¼ cups / 450 g granulated sugar
- 2 tsp baking powder
- 1 cup / 240 ml sunflower oil
- ¾ cup /180 ml water
- Blanched almonds or whole cloves, for garnish

Filling/topping

- 3 tbsp sunflower oil
- 4½ cups / 680 g pitted dates, chopped
- 1 tsp ground cinnamon
- ⅛ tsp ground cloves

Syrup

- 1 cup / 200 g caster sugar
- ½ cup / 120ml water
- 1 cup / 240 ml clear honey
- 2-3 tbsp lemon juice

Heat the oven to 340°F/170°C/Gas Mark 3. Oil a 12-inch/30-cm square cake pan.

1. Heat the oil in a heavy skillet or copper-bottom pan.
2. Add the chopped dates and cook over a low heat, stirring continuously for about 20 minutes, until the dates form a thick paste.
3. Remove the pan from the heat and stir in the cinnamon and cloves. Set aside and allow the paste to cool.
4. In a large bowl, combine the semolina, baking powder and granulated sugar.
5. Stir in the sunflower oil and water and beat until the mixture forms a thick batter.
6. Pour half the batter into the greased cake pan.
7. Add the date filling on top of the mixture, pressing it into the corners of the pan so it covers the whole surface, and top with the remaining mixture.
8. Bake for 35 minutes, or until golden brown and a skewer inserted in the middle comes out clean.
9. To make the syrup, combine all the ingredients in a saucepan and bring them to a simmer over a low heat.
10. Cook, stirring frequently, for about 10 minutes, or until all the sugar has dissolved and the mixture has thickened.
11. Pour the hot syrup over the cake and then set aside for the syrup to be absorbed.
12. Allow the cake to cool completely then stand it at room temperature for at least six hours before slicing and serving.

MOROCCO

Meskouta with Orange Juice

prep 10 mins/bake 40 mins

Meskouta was originally the cake of the Moroccan poor – it contains no butter because that was expensive and hard to come by, especially under French colonial rule. It was then sometimes cooked in a pot over a brazier rather than in an oven. Nowadays it is often known as 'winter cake' because this is when citrus fruits are in season. This is a very simple recipe with few ingredients but it results in a delicious, soft cake. It is also, not surprisingly, very orangey.

- 4 eggs
- 1½ cups /300 g caster sugar
- ½ cup / 120 ml vegetable oil
- 2 cups / 260 g all-purpose/plain flour
- 4 tsp baking powder
- ½ tsp salt
- ½ cup / 120 ml fresh orange juice
- zest from 2 oranges
- 1 tsp vanilla extract

Heat oven to 355°F/180°C/Gas Mark 4.

Grease and flour a bundt or tube pan (a round pan with a hole in the middle).

1. In a medium bowl, beat together the eggs and sugar until the mixture is pale and creamy.
2. Gradually beat in the vegetable oil.
3. Stir in the flour, baking powder and salt until it is completely combined.
4. Add the orange juice and beat until the mixture is smooth.
5. Add the orange zest and vanilla extract and stir well.
6. Pour the batter into the prepared tin.
7. Place in a preheated oven for 40 minutes until golden brown, or until a skewer inserted in the middle comes out clean.
8. Allow the cake to cool in the pan for 10 minutes, then invert onto a rack to finish cooling.

PALESTINE

Almond & Citrus Olive Oil Cake

prep 10 mins/bake 30-40 mins

This recipe was provided by one of New Internationalist's fair-trade suppliers, Zaytoun, which was formed as a community-interest company in 2004 to seek overseas markets for artisan Palestinian food products, including olive oil and almonds, which are both among the ingredients here. The almonds and oranges complement each other really well in this wonderfully moist cake, while the thick layer of almonds on the top adds to the luxurious sensation.

1 cup / 130 g all-purpose/plain flour
½ cup / 60 g ground almonds
1½ tsp baking powder
1 tsp salt
3 large eggs, beaten
¾ cup / 150 g caster sugar
½ cup / 120 ml extra-virgin olive oil
½ tsp vanilla extract
grated zest of 2 oranges
½ cup / 120 ml fresh squeezed orange juice
⅓ cup / 60 g flaked almonds
Confectioner's/icing sugar for dusting

Heat the oven to 355°F/180°C/Gas 4.
Grease and flour a 9-inch/23-cm round cake pan.

1. In a bowl, mix together the flour, ground almonds, baking powder and salt.
2. In a separate bowl, beat the eggs, caster sugar and olive oil until thoroughly combined.
3. Add the vanilla extract, orange zest and orange juice.
4. Gradually add the dry ingredients into the mixture and beat until the batter is smooth and creamy.
5. Pour the batter into the cake pan and sprinkle thickly with flaked almonds
6. Bake for 30-40 minutes or until a skewer inserted in the middle comes out clean.
7. Allow the cake to cool in the pan for 10 minutes before removing to cool it completely on a rack. Dust with icing sugar before serving.

ISRAEL

Eretz Yisrael

prep 30 mins/bake 40 mins

Until I baked this cake I didn't realize how well marzipan and oranges complement each other. Marzipan was used in the Middle East as early as the fifth century and there is a long history of this ingredient in Jewish baking. Including it in the body of the cake is unusual for Western tastes but it works so well that I will be doing it again. The dates may sink despite all your best efforts – don't worry, you won't get any complaints!

¾ cup / 150 g caster sugar
Grated zest of 2 oranges
½ cup / 120 g marzipan, chopped to the texture of gravel
4 eggs
1 tsp baking powder
¼ tsp salt
⅓ cup / 50 g candied citrus peel, chopped
1¾ cups / 200 g all-purpose/plain flour
½ cup / 100 g pitted dates, finely chopped
¼ cup /60 ml fresh orange juice
¾ cup / 170 g melted, unsalted butter

Heat the oven to 355°F/180°C/Gas Mark 4.
Grease a 9-inch/23-cm spring-form pan. Line the bottom of the pan with parchment paper and grease again.

1. In a bowl, combine the sugar, chopped marzipan and orange zest.
2. Add the eggs and whisk for at least three minutes, until light and fluffy and pale yellow in color.
3. Take three tablespoons of the flour and sprinkle over the dates and candied citrus peel in a small bowl. Set aside. The flour coating can help to prevent them from sinking to the bottom of the batter.
4. Sift the remaining flour, the baking powder, and salt and mix thoroughly.
5. Add the orange juice and melted butter and mix until the dry ingredients are incorporated and the batter is soft and creamy. Take care not to over-mix.
6. Fold in the floured dates and citrus peel.
7. Pour the batter into the spring-form cake tin, tapping it on a hard surface a couple of times to remove the air bubbles,
8. Bake on the middle rack of the oven for 40 minutes or until a skewer inserted in the middle comes out clean.
9. Remove from oven and leave for 10 minutes before taking out of the pan and removing the greaseproof paper. When completely cooled, sprinkle lightly with icing sugar if desired.

KUWAIT

Arabic Honey Cake

prep 20 mins/bake 30-35 mins

Taking a cake out of the oven halfway through baking to add another element seems an odd thing to do but I can assure you that it works with this recipe. The golden brown, shiny topping cools to a soft toffee consistency with a crunch provided by the almonds. Once you start eating it is difficult to stop...

- ⅓ cup / 80 g butter, melted
- 3 eggs
- ½ cup / 100 g caster sugar
- ½ tsp vanilla extract
- ½ tsp baking powder
- ½ cup / 65 g + 1 tbsp all-purpose/plain flour

Topping

- ½ cup / 115 g butter
- ½ cup / 100 g caster sugar
- ⅓ cup / 80 ml honey
- ½ cup / 90 g slivered almonds
- ½ tsp cinnamon

Heat the oven to 375°F/190°C/Gas Mark 5.
Grease a 10-inch/25.5-cm round cake pan.

1. Beat the eggs, sugar and vanilla until the mixture is pale and creamy.
2. Add the melted butter and mix well.
3. Sift the flour and baking powder into the mixture and combine gently.
4. Pour the mixture into the pan and bake for 12 minutes.
5. In a small saucepan on a medium heat, melt the butter.
6. Add the sugar, honey, sliced almonds and cinnamon, stirring constantly until the almonds are completely covered.
7. Remove the cake from the oven and pour the topping onto the cake. Return it to the oven for another 15-20 minutes or until it is golden brown.
8. Allow to cool completely in the pan.

SYRIA

Walnut-Semolina Cake with Figs

Wheat free

prep 20 mins/bake 45 mins

I do like cakes that have a contrast of textures and this is one of them. The other ingredients are quite plain and there are no spices but somehow the roasted walnuts and figs provide a distinct flavor. Keep an eye on the walnuts while they are roasting – as soon as they produce a fragrance, take them out. The honey in the mixture also gives it warmth and contributes to the glazed surface. The cake can be stored in an airtight container at room temperature for up to three days.

- 1½ cups /160 g walnut halves
- 1 cup / 180 g semolina flour
- 1½ tsp baking powder
- ½ tsp salt
- ¾ cup / 170 g unsalted butter, softened
- ½ cup / 120 ml honey
- ¼ cup / 50 g caster sugar
- 3 large eggs, at room temperature
- ½ tsp pure vanilla extract
- ⅓ cup / 80 g dried figs, finely chopped

Heat the oven to 355°F/180°C/Gas Mark 4.

Grease a 9-inch/23-cm round cake pan. Line the bottom of the pan with wax paper and grease again. Flour the pan, tapping out the excess.

1. Spread the walnut halves on a baking tray and toast them in the oven for about 8-10 minutes until fragrant and golden brown. Let them cool completely or they will turn into an oily paste when ground up.
2. Finely grind the walnuts and mix with the semolina flour, baking powder and salt. Set aside.
3. In a large bowl, beat the butter with the honey and sugar until light and fluffy, which will take about three minutes.
4. Add the eggs one at a time, beating well between additions.
5. Add the vanilla extract.
6. At low speed, beat in the semolina flour mixture.
7. Add the chopped figs and stir through the mixture until evenly distributed.
8. Pour the batter into the prepared pan and bake the cake on the middle rack of the oven for 45 minutes (check after 35 minutes), or until a skewer inserted in the middle comes out clean.
9. Let the cake cool in the pan for 10 minutes, then turn it out onto a wire rack to cool completely. Peel off the wax paper and invert the cake onto a large serving plate.

CAKE LIST

Europe

RECIPES FROM...

Norway

Finland

Denmark

Holland

Poland

Wales

Germany

Czech Republic

Hungary

Switzerland

Romania

Italy

Spain

Greece

FINLAND

Kermakuku

Sour cream cake

prep 15 mins/bake 1 hour

While this is quite a plain cake, it is beautifully moist and flavorsome. The recipe is very easy to follow. As you will see from the photograph, I made a small amount of glacé icing to decorate the cake but, if you preferred, you could simply sprinkle confectioner's/icing sugar on top. This would be a quick cake to bake when you are going to be invaded at short notice by friends and family for tea.

2 eggs, beaten
2 cups / 400 g caster sugar
2 cups / 480 ml sour cream
2-3 drops almond extract
½ teaspoon ground cardamom
2¾ cups / 360 g all-purpose/plain flour
½ tsp salt
1 tsp baking powder
½ tsp cinnamon

Grease and flour a large bundt or tube cake pan (circular, with a hole in the middle) and sprinkle with granulated sugar.

Heat the oven to 355°F/180°C/Gas Mark 4.

1. In a large bowl, whisk together the eggs, sugar, sour cream, almond extract and ground cardamom.
2. Sift the flour, salt, baking powder and cinnamon into the creamed mixture and combine thoroughly.
3. Pour the mixture into the prepared cake pan.
4. Bake for one hour or until a skewer inserted in the middle comes out clean.
5. Allow the cake to cool before removing it from the pan.
6. When it is completely cool, either sprinkle confectioner's/icing sugar or drizzle glacé icing over the cake.

GREECE

Melaxrini

Wheat free

prep 20 mins/bake 50-60 mins/syrup 30 mins

This makes a change from the baklava that usually represents Greece. Watching the mixture swell in the oven is quite entertaining and the resulting cake has a good combination of soft and crunchy textures. It is a good idea to cut this into small slices to ensure that everyone is able to try it as it is impossible to have too much of this cake!

10 eggs, separated
1 cup / 200 g caster sugar
⅔ cup / 100 g finely chopped walnuts
7 tbsp semolina flour
3 tbsp finely ground breadcrumbs
1 tsp ground cinnamon
1 tsp ground cloves

Syrup
3 cups / 720 ml water
3 cups / 600 g caster sugar
1 tsp vanilla extract

Heat the oven to 355°F/180°C/Gas Mark 4.
Grease a high-sided 8-inch/20-cm square cake pan.

1. Whisk the egg yolks with the sugar until they are light and fluffy.
2. Add the cinnamon, cloves, ground walnuts, semolina flour and breadcrumbs until all the ingredients are combined.
3. In a separate bowl, beat the egg whites until they form firm peaks then gradually add to the mixture, folding in gently with a spatula in one direction. Do not over-mix.
4. Pour the cake mix into the high-sided cake pan.
5. Bake the cake for 50-60 minutes or until a skewer inserted in the middle comes out clean.
6. Allow the cake to cool completely.
7. Boil the sugar, water and vanilla extract for 30 minutes.
8. Insert a fine skewer at many different points, all over the surface of the cake.
9. Gradually pour the hot syrup over the cake. The holes will allow the syrup to soak through.

GERMANY

Schwarzwäldertorte

Black Forest Gâteau (see photo overleaf)

prep 90 mins/bake 15 mins

This lovely gâteau went out of fashion for some reason and that may have been because it has been changed over time to a sticky, over-sweet concoction. This recipe is more true to the original. It has a grown-up flavor provided by the kirsch (do not use cherry brandy or liqueur) while the sour cherries balance the sweetness of the butter-cream filling. The sponge is really light and it's a challenge to introduce sufficient air to make it rise as there is no raising agent, so be prepared to stand and whip the mixture for at least 10 minutes. The effort will go some way towards balancing the calories contained in this special cake!

6 large eggs
1 cup / 200 g caster sugar
1 tsp vanilla extract
1 cup / 120 g unsweetened baking chocolate, melted
1½ cups / 195 g all-purpose/plain flour, sifted

Syrup
¼ cup / 50 g caster sugar
⅓ cup / 80 ml water
2 tbsp kirsch

Filling
3 cups / 400 g confectioner's/icing sugar
⅔ cup / 160 g unsalted butter
2 egg yolks
3 tbsp kirsch
2 cups / 600 g sour cherries, drained and patted dry. Keep 6 cherries back for the topping.

Topping
2 tbsp confectioner's/icing sugar
1 cup / 240 ml heavy/double cream, whipped
Unsweetened chocolate for decoration

Thoroughly grease (use butter) and flour three 8-inch/20-cm cake pans (even if the pans are non-stick).

Heat the oven to 355°F/180°C/Gas Mark 4.

1. In a large bowl, beat the eggs, sugar and vanilla extract together for about 10 minutes, until thick and fluffy.
2. Fold the flour and melted chocolate alternately into the egg mixture, ending with an addition of flour.
3. Divide the batter equally between the three cake pans.
4. Bake for 10 to 15 minutes or until a skewer inserted in the middle comes out clean.
5. Allow the cakes to cool in the pans for 5 minutes; then carefully turn them out on racks and allow them to cool completely.

Syrup

1. To make the syrup, mix together the sugar and water in a small saucepan, and boil for 5 minutes.
2. When the syrup has cooled, stir in the kirsch.
3. Prick the cake layers and pour syrup over all three of them.

Filling

1. To make the butter-cream filling, beat together the sugar and butter in a bowl until they are well blended.
2. Add the egg yolk and continue to beat the mixture until light and fluffy, which will take about 5 minutes.
3. Fold in the kirsch.
4. To assemble, place one layer of sponge on a cake plate.
5. Spread with butter-cream filling, then drop half of the cherries evenly over the cream.
6. Place the second layer on the cake and add butter cream and cherries as before.
7. Place the third layer on top.

Topping

1. Fold the confectioner's/icing sugar into the whipped cream and then cover the sides and top of the cake with the whipped-cream mixture. Keep a little cream back if you intend to ice rosettes on the top.
2. Decorate the top of the cake with the remaining cherries and grated or curled chocolate.

Chill until serving time and store in a refrigerator.

HUNGARY

Sutemeny Rigo Jancsi

Chocolate Mousse Cake (see photo previous page)

prep 45 mins/bake 15 mins

This cake is named after a 19th-century Hungarian Romani violinist who seduced and married Clara Ward, a wealthy American socialite and wife of the Belgian Prince de Caraman-Chimay. Rigo devised the cake with the help of a chef and, to be honest, I can quite see why she fell for it and for him! It's a real choc fest – but do use really high-quality chocolate. The crunchy base complements the smooth mousse and the tot of rum gives it yet another kick – as if this were needed.

¾ cups / 175 g unsalted butter, softened
½ cup / 100 g caster sugar, divided into 2 x 50g portions
⅓ cup / 85 g dark chocolate, melted and cooled to lukewarm
4 eggs, separated
Pinch salt
½ cup / 65 g all-purpose/plain flour

Filling

1½ cups / 285 g milk chocolate, chopped
1½ cups / 360 ml heavy/double cream
2 tbsp dark rum
1 tsp vanilla extract

Glaze

1 cup / 200 g milk chocolate, chopped
2 tbsp unsalted butter
2 tbsp corn syrup/golden syrup
1 tsp vanilla extract

Heat the oven to 355°F/180°C/Gas Mark 4.

Grease and line a 13-inch/33-cm x 9-inch/23-cm jelly/swiss roll pan with parchment paper.

1. In a large bowl, cream the butter with half the sugar until light and fluffy.
2. Add the cooled melted chocolate.
3. Beat in the egg yolks gradually. Set aside.
4. In a medium bowl, beat the egg whites and salt until the mixture thickens. Add the other half of the sugar and beat until stiff peaks form.
5. Gradually and carefully stir the whipped egg whites into the chocolate mixture, one-third at a time.
6. Sprinkle the flour over the mixture, carefully folding in so that the volume is not reduced.
7. Pour the mixture into the prepared pan and bake for 12-15 minutes, or until the cake starts to pull away from the sides. Take care not to overbake.
8. Allow the cake to cool in its pan on a rack for a few minutes. Then place the cake rack over the cake, hold firmly and turn the cake upside down, out of the pan and on to the rack. Remove the parchment paper and allow the cake to cool completely.

Filling

1. While the cake is cooling, place the chopped milk chocolate in a heatproof bowl. Set aside.
2. Bring the cream to a boil in a saucepan or in the microwave. Pour it over the chocolate.
3. Cover with plastic wrap and let it stand for 10 minutes.
4. Add the rum and vanilla, and stir until smooth.
5. Refrigerate the mixture for 1 hour.
6. Remove from the refrigerator and whisk until the volume has doubled.
7. Now take the cake out of the fridge, cut it in half and place one half on a serving plate.
8. Spread the filling over the cake and top with the remaining cake half.
9. Refrigerate again for 1 hour.

Glaze

1. While the cake is in the refrigerator, place the chopped chocolate, butter and syrup in a heatproof bowl over a saucepan of just boiling water. Over a medium heat, stir until the ingredients have melted. Remove from heat.
2. Add the vanilla and continue to stir until smooth. Let the mixture cool for 10 minutes.
3. Pour the glaze evenly over the cake, using a spatula to cover the sides if necessary. When the cake is completely covered, refrigerate for 30 minutes or until the glaze is set.
4. Cut into small squares before serving as this cake is so rich. Any leftovers should be refrigerated – though this is unlikely to be an issue!

ETHERLANDS

Pruimencake

Plum Cake

prep 20 mins/bake 35 mins

This is such an easy cake to make but the brilliant pink of the cooked plums makes it look impressive. It will work just as well using other fruits for the topping such as peaches or persimmons and is a good way of using up any combination of over-ripe soft fruits left over in the fruit bowl. This is one of those cakes that can also be eaten as a dessert with cream or ice cream.

1 cup / 130 g sifted all-purpose/plain flour
1½ tsp baking powder
¼ tsp salt
½ cup /100 g caster sugar
¼ cup / 55 g butter
1 egg
¼ cup / 60 ml milk
5 pitted ripe plums, sliced into eighths

Topping
1 tsp cinnamon
¼ tsp nutmeg
3 tbsp caster sugar
3 tbsp butter, melted

Syrup
⅓ cup redcurrant jelly or apricot jam
1 tbsp hot water

Heat the oven to 375°F/190°C/Gas Mark 5.
Grease a 12-inch/30-cm x 8-inch/20-cm baking dish that is 2 inches/5 cm deep.

1 In a bowl, sift together the flour, baking powder, and salt. Add sugar.
2 Chop the butter into the flour and rub in until the mix resembles large breadcrumbs.
3 In a small bowl, beat together the egg and milk and then stir gradually into the flour mixture. Work into a sticky dough.
4 Spread the dough into the base of the greased baking dish.
6 Arrange the sliced plums in overlapping rows on top of the dough. Set aside.
7 For the topping, combine the melted butter, sugar, cinnamon and nutmeg and then spoon the mixture over the sliced plums.
8 Bake for 35 minutes, or until the plums are tender.
9 While the cake is cooling, mix the jelly or jam with hot water to make a thick syrup. Brush over the fruit. Cut into squares and serve while still warm.

ITALY

Castagnaccio

Wheat free/Vegan

Chestnut Cake

prep 10 mins/bake 45 mins

This is so simple and quick to make and results in a rich, dense cake with a strong, 'adult' taste. It is slightly sweetened by the sultanas but is made to be eaten with sweet things such as cream or crème fraîche and is traditionally accompanied by a sweet wine such as Vin Santo. The smooth texture, which has a distinctive chestnut flavor, is offset by the crunch of the pine nuts and the slight aroma of rosemary.

½ cup / 120 ml sweet or dessert wine
5½ cups / 600 g chestnut flour
6 tbsp olive oil
1 tsp finely chopped candied orange
Pinch of salt
½ cup / 70 g raisins
2 cups / 480 ml water
¼ cup / 40 g pine nuts
a few rosemary leaves

Lightly grease a 9-inch/23-cm spring-release pan.
Heat the oven to 375°F/190°C/Gas Mark 5.

1. Place the raisins and sweet wine in a small saucepan and heat to boiling. Remove from the heat and allow the raisins to plump for 10 minutes, then drain and discard the wine.
2. In a large bowl, combine the chestnut flour, 4 tablespoons of olive oil, candied orange, salt, raisins and the water.
3. Whisk until the mixture is smooth and until it has the consistency of a thick batter, carefully adding additional water if required.
4. Pour into the prepared pan and sprinkle the pine nuts and rosemary leaves on the top.
5. Drizzle with the remaining two tablespoons of olive oil and bake for about 45 minutes or until the cake is set, lightly browned and cracked on top or until a skewer inserted in the middle comes out clean.
6. Allow the cake to cool slightly before removing from the pan.
7. Serve cold in small slices.

POLAND

Jablecznik

Apple Cake

prep 20 mins/bake 40 mins

The cloves smell wonderful while this cake is cooking and they also complement the flavor of the apples. The result is surprisingly tasty considering that there are no added spices but if you like cinnamon with your apples, you can sprinkle this over lightly when arranging the apple slices on the batter. Serve cold – or hot with cream.

- 2⅓ cups / 300 g all-purpose/plain flour
- 2½ tsp baking powder
- ½ tsp salt
- 1 cup / 200 g caster sugar
- ½ cup / 115 g butter, softened
- 1½ oz / 40 g butter, cold and cut into pieces
- ¾ cup /180 ml milk
- 2 large eggs
- 4 large apples, peeled, cored and thinly sliced
- ¼ tsp cloves
- 1 tbsp caster sugar

Lightly grease a 13-inch/33-cm x 9-inch/23-cm baking pan. Heat the oven to 355°F/180°C/Gas Mark 4.

1. In a large bowl, combine the flour, baking powder, salt and three-quarters of the sugar.
2. Add the softened butter, milk and eggs and beat well until creamy.
3. Pour half the batter into the prepared pan, then layer on half of the sliced apples.
4. Keep about half a cup of batter back then spoon the remaining batter over the apples, covering them completely.
5. Arrange the remaining slices on top and dot the reserved half-cup of batter over the apples.
6. In a bowl, rub in the sugar, cloves and cold butter until the mixture resembles coarse breadcrumbs. Sprinkle over the mixture in the cake pan.
7. Bake for 40 minutes or until a skewer inserted in the middle comes out clean.
8. Remove the cake from the oven and sprinkle it with caster sugar while it is still hot.
9. Leave in the pan for 10-15 minutes to allow the juices from the cooked apple to soak into the cake.
10. Cut into squares.

NORWAY

Almond Cake with Custard Glaze

Gluten free

prep 15 mins/bake 30 mins/glaze 15 mins

This is a light almond cake with a rich custard glaze. The glaze takes a lot longer than the cake itself to make, mainly because it should be refrigerated for at least four hours. I drizzled melted chocolate over the custard to give it more of a party look but the cake tastes just as good without.

5 egg whites
1½ cups / 200 g confectioner's/icing sugar
1 tsp baking powder
2 cups / 200 g ground almonds

Topping
5 egg yolks
⅔ cup / 130 g caster sugar
½ cup / 120 ml heavy/double cream
½ cup / 115 g butter

Heat the oven to 390°F/200°C/Gas Mark 6.
Grease a 9-inch/23-cm spring-form pan.

1. In a bowl, whip the egg whites with an electric mixer until firm peaks are formed. Set aside.
2. In a separate bowl, combine the ground almonds, baking powder and confectioner's/icing sugar.
3. Fold the egg whites into the almond mixture in three additions.
4. Pour the batter into the prepared pan and bake for 25 minutes or until the top of the cake springs back when pressed lightly.
5. Allow the cake to cool in the pan for 10 minutes then remove onto a cooling rack.
6. In a heatproof or metal bowl set over a pan of simmering water, whisk together the egg yolks and sugar until pale and creamy.
7. Stir in the double cream. Continue to cook and stir until the mixture thickens into a custard.
8. Remove from the heat, and stir in the butter until it is completely melted and mixed in.
9. Cover the bowl in plastic wrap and refrigerate, preferably overnight but for at least 4 hours.
10. Spread the topping over the cake and decorate as required.

CZECH REPUBLIC

Buchty (see photo overleaf)

prep 3 hours/bake 30 mins

These sweet buns are great for making with children and for putting in their lunch boxes. The buns are traditionally filled with poppy seeds mixed with a solid cottage cheese, which can be found in Polish supermarkets, although if you can't find that a good alternative would be to use mascarpone. The buns would be just as tasty if you filled them with your favorite jam, with chocolate spread or with stewed fruit.

3 tbsp caster sugar
1 cup / 180 ml lukewarm milk
6 tsp / 20 g dried yeast
3½ cups / 450 g all-purpose/plain flour
2½ tsp / 10 g vanilla sugar
1 pinch salt
⅓ cup / 75 g chopped unsalted butter (at room temperature)
2 large eggs, separated
1 tbsp lemon juice
Finely grated peel of 1 lemon

Filling

either 2 tbsp / 50 g plum compote
or ½ cup / 100 g Polish soft cheese (see above) or mascarpone
1 tbsp confectioner's/icing sugar
2½ tbsp poppy seeds
1 tbsp milk

A little confectioner's/icing sugar for dusting
1 beaten egg for coating

Grease an 8-inch/20-cm x 10-inch/25-cm baking pan (a lasagne dish could also be used).

Heat the oven to 375ºF/190ºC/Gas Mark 5.

1 In a small bowl, mix one tablespoon of sugar into the lukewarm milk and add the yeast. Leave in a warm place for about 20 minutes to let the yeast rise. It will be ready when it has produced a bubbling foam on the surface of the liquid.
2 Place the flour, the rest of the sugar, vanilla sugar and salt in a large bowl and mix well.
3 Add the chopped butter and lightly rub into the flour.
4 Beat the egg yolks in a separate bowl and then add them, the bubbling yeast mixture and the lemon juice and the zest to the flour mixture.
5 Using your hands, mix until all the ingredients are combined into a soft dough. You may need to add a little more flour at this stage but be careful not to add too much at once or the dough will be dry and heavy.
6 Knead the dough on a floured surface until it is completely smooth, then place in a ceramic or glass bowl and cover with a clean cloth. Allow the dough to prove in a warm space for 2-3 hours or until it has doubled in size.

7. While the dough is rising, combine the curd cheese, confectioner's/icing sugar, poppy seeds and milk, and beat well until smooth.
8. When the dough has risen to twice its size, tip out of the bowl on to a lightly floured surface. Using a dessert spoon, divide the dough into 20 pieces. This is a good measure of the size of the ball of dough required to make a buchty.
9. Roll each piece of dough into a ball, then, using your fingertips, shape the dough into a flat circle about 4 inches / 10 cm across.
10. Place a teaspoon of either the curd cheese filling or the plum compote in the middle of each circle and then seal the edges by pinching the dough together, tucking the ends under the buchty to ensure the filling does not leak out during cooking. Take care not to overfill.
11. Brush the sides of each bun with melted butter to prevent them sticking to each other.
12. Place the filled buns alongside each other in the baking dish with no gaps between them.
13. Cover them with a clean cloth and leave to rise for a further 15 minutes.
14. Brush the buns with beaten egg and bake on the lower rack of the oven for 30 minutes.
15. Remove the buchty buns from the oven and leave them to cool in the dish for 10 minutes before transferring them to a wire rack to cool completely.
16. Dust with sieved confectioner's/icing sugar.

DENMARK

Valmuefrø Kage

Poppy-Seed Cake (see photo previous page)

prep 40 mins/bake 30 mins

Every part of this cake is delectable – although the sponge is feather light, the poppy seeds and hazelnuts give a satisfying crunch. The custard filling is tasty and the rum topping gives the whole confection a grown-up flavor. It would be particularly good to eat along with a cup of coffee. I gave the hazelnuts for the custard filling an extra whizz in the food processor for a finer texture but left them a little more roughly ground for the topping.

¾ cup / 160 g soft butter
1½ cups / 300 g caster sugar
2 cups / 260 g all-purpose/plain flour, sifted
2 tsp baking powder
½ tsp salt
½ cup / 75 g poppy seeds (soak the poppy seeds in the milk and vanilla overnight)
1 cup / 240 ml milk
1 tsp vanilla extract
4 egg whites

Filling
4 egg yolks
¾ cup / 150 g caster sugar
2 tbsp corn starch/cornflour
¼ tsp salt
1½ cups / 360 ml milk
½ cup / 55 g hazelnuts, finely ground
1 tsp vanilla paste

Topping
1 cup / 135 g confectioner's/icing sugar
3 tbsp rum
½ cup / 55 g hazelnuts, ground

Heat the oven to 355°F/180°C/Gas Mark 4. Grease and lightly flour 2 x 8-inch/20-cm sponge cake pans.

1. Beat butter until light and creamy.
2. Add the sugar gradually and continue to beat well. Set aside.
3. Sift the flour, baking powder and salt together.
4. Add a third of the flour mixture and a third of the milk/poppy-seed mixture to the creamed butter mix, alternating until all the mixtures are used and blending well after each addition.
5. Whip the egg whites until stiff and fold into the mixture.
6. Divide the mixture equally between the prepared cake pans and bake for 25 minutes or until the top is golden brown and a skewer inserted in the middle comes out clean.
7. Allow the cakes to cool for about 10 minutes before turning out onto a cooling rack.

Filling

1. In a heat-proof bowl, beat the egg yolks until frothy.
2. Add the sugar, corn starch/cornflour and salt and gradually add the milk, stirring until all ingredients are combined.
3. Place the bowl on top of a pan of boiling water, taking care not to get any water in the mixture and to keep sufficient water in the base of the pan.
4. Stir constantly to keep the mixture from scorching and until the mixture has thickened and absorbed all the milk. Remove it from the heat.
5. Add the ground hazelnuts and vanilla paste. Mix the filling well, and spread it between the cake layers when they have completely cooled.

Topping

1. Gradually add the rum to the confectioner's/icing sugar, stirring until the icing is smooth.
2. Cover the top and sides of the cake.
3. Sprinkle the ground hazelnuts over the top.

Bündner Nusstorte

prep 40 mins/bake 35-40 mins

This pie has found its way into a cake book because it is delicious and really interesting to make. The sugar takes 20-30 minutes to caramelize but watching it go through several stages of metamorphosis before turning into a golden toffee is fascinating. Make sure the pastry is cold before rolling it out, as it is delicate and a little sticky – try to work it as little as possible. Take care to seal the pastry well as the challenge is to stop the filling from bubbling out when the pie is baked. Serve hot or cold, on its own or with cream.

- 2¼ cups / 300 g all-purpose/plain flour
- ¾ cup / 150 g caster sugar
- ⅔ cup / 150 g butter, chilled
- 1 egg, beaten and mixed with a little milk
- ¼ tsp salt

Filling

- 1½ cups / 300 g caster sugar
- 10 tsp / 50 ml water
- 2 cups / 250 g roughly chopped walnuts
- ¾ cup + 4 tsp / 200 ml heavy/double cream
- 1 dessert spoon of honey

Heat the oven to 355°F/180°C/Gas Mark 4. Grease a 9-inch/23-cm spring-form pan.

1. In a bowl, rub the butter into the flour and salt until it resembles fine breadcrumbs.
2. Add the sugar and combine well.
3. Add the beaten egg and work into a dough, handling as little as possible.
4. Wrap the dough in plastic wrap/cling film and refrigerate for at least half an hour.
5. While the dough is chilling, in a heavy-based saucepan and over a medium heat, combine the sugar and water. Stir constantly until the mixture dissolves to a golden brown caramel liquid – this will take about 25 minutes.
6. Add the chopped walnuts, cream and honey, stirring well to ensure the walnuts are completely covered. Remove the mixture from the heat and allow it to cool to room temperature.
7. Divide the chilled dough into two portions of two-thirds and one-third. To prevent sticking, lightly flour the work surface and the rolling pin. Roll out the larger portion to a 13-inch/33-cm diameter circle and use this to line the base of the spring-form pan, gently pressing the pastry against the sides.
8. Pour the cooled walnut cream mixture into the pie base.
9. Roll out the remaining pastry, brush the edge of the base with egg/milk mixture to seal it before placing the lid on the pie. Trim off the excess pastry and brush the surface with the remaining egg mixture.
10. Bake for 35-40 minutes or until the pastry is a golden brown.
11. Leave the pie to cool until it is lukewarm in the pan, then loosen the sides, release the clip and carefully transfer the pie to a wire rack to cool completely.

ROMANIA

Marble Cake

prep 10 mins/bake 35 mins

This marble cake is quick and easy to make. Take care not to over-mix the plain and the chocolate batters or you will end up with a streaky, light-brown cake! As an optional extra, you could decorate the top with fruit and nuts.

4 eggs
2 cups / 400 g caster sugar
1 cup / 240 ml milk
1 cup / 240 ml vegetable oil (not olive)
2 cups / 260 g all-purpose/plain flour
2 tsp baking powder
½ tsp salt
2 tsp vanilla extract
zest of 2 lemons
3 tbsp cocoa powder

Grease two loaf pans, and line with greaseproof paper. Heat the oven to 355°F/180°C/Gas Mark 4.

1. In a bowl, beat the eggs, sugar, lemon zest and vanilla extract until the mixture is creamy.
2. Add the milk and oil and beat until the batter is smooth.
3. Sift the flour, baking powder and salt into the mixture, and stir until combined.
4. Divide the batter into two portions.
5. Mix one portion with the cocoa powder.
6. Pour the plain batter into the loaf pans and pour the cocoa batter over the top.
7. Drag a skewer through the mixture once or twice.
8. Bake for about 40 minutes or until a skewer inserted in the middle comes out clean.

SPAIN

Tarta de Santiago

Wheat free/Gluten free

St James' Cake

prep 15 min/bake 45 min

Tarta de Santiago is a traditional cake that is popular in the Galicia region of northwest Spain and is named for the country's patron saint, St James. It is dense and moist, with a rich almond flavor, and is perfect with a cup of coffee. For the decoration, I downloaded an outline of the cross of St James and cut it out of cardboard. Once the cake was completely cooled I placed it on the centre of the cake and sprinkled the surface with confectioner's/icing sugar.

2½ cups / 250 g ground almonds
1¼ cups / 250 g caster sugar
5 eggs
Zest of 1 lemon
½ tsp cinnamon
Confectioner's/icing sugar for sprinkling

Heat the oven to 355°F/180°C/Gas Mark 4.
Grease and flour an 8-inch/20-cm spring-form pan.

1. In a bowl, mix the sugar, ground almonds, cinnamon and lemon zest until thoroughly combined. Set aside.
2. In a separate bowl, whisk the eggs until frothy. Add the almond mixture and stir until thoroughly combined.
3. Pour the mixture into the prepared pan and bake for 45 minutes until the surface is toasted and golden or when a skewer inserted in the middle comes out clean.
4. Allow the cake to cool completely in the pan before releasing.
5. When the cake is cold, put your stencil of the cross of St James on the surface and sieve the confectioner's/icing sugar evenly across the cake. Remove the stencil carefully, taking care not to spill sugar onto the design.

WALES

Bara Brith

prep 20 mins/bake 90 mins

How is it that this traditional Welsh recipe, which is so simple to make and which contains so few ingredients, results in such a rich-tasting fruit loaf? It's even better when served with butter, it's great for lunch boxes and it keeps extremely well in an airtight container. All in all, this is a really useful cake.

1½ cups / 350 ml brewed tea, cooled
2 cups / 340 g mixed dried fruit, soaked overnight in the tea
1⅓ cups / 200 g soft brown sugar
2⅓ cups / 300 g cake/self-raising flour
1 egg

Heat the oven to 355°F/180°C/ Gas Mark 4.

1. In a large bowl, add the sugar and mixed fruit to the cold tea and leave this to soak overnight.
2. Add the flour and egg to the tea mixture and stir until the mixture is smooth.
3. Line a loaf tin with non-stick baking parchment and pour the mixture in.
4. Bake for 90 minutes. Towards the end of baking, check every 10 minutes with a knife or skewer to see if all the mixture is cooked.
5. Once cooled, slice and serve topped with butter.

CAKE LIST

South & East Asia

RECIPES FROM...

Afghanistan

China

Japan

India

Taiwan

Cambodia

Sri Lanka

Philippines

Malaysia

INDIA

Mango Cake

Vegan

prep 20 mins/bake 30-40 mins

Simple recipes and fresh ingredients often give the best results and this Indian cake is a case in point. The mango not only comes through strongly in the flavor but also enhances the color of the cake. Use well ripened mangoes and keep a few slices back for decorating. This is a wonderful summer cake.

1½ cups / 195 g all-purpose/plain flour
½ tsp salt
1 tsp cardamom powder
2 tsp baking powder
1½ cups / 350 ml mango purée (from 4-5 fresh mangoes)
⅓ cup / 80 ml vegetable oil
⅔ cup / 130 g granulated sugar
1 tsp vanilla extract
Slices of mango and mint leaves for decoration

Heat the oven to 355°F/180°C/Gas Mark 4.
Oil a 9-inch/23-cm square cake pan.

1. Sieve the flour, salt, cardamom powder and baking powder together. Set aside.
2. In a separate bowl, combine the mango purée, vegetable oil, sugar and vanilla and whisk well until smooth.
3. Gradually add the dry ingredients, mixing carefully with each addition. Do not over-beat the mixture as this may increase the density of the cake.
4. Pour into the greased cake pan.
5. Bake for 30-40 minutes or until a skewer inserted in the middle comes out clean.
6. When the cake has cooled, dust it with confectioner's/icing sugar and garnish with slices or chunks of fresh mango and mint leaves.

MALAYSIA

Bolu Sarang Semut

Honeycomb Cake

prep 25 mins/bake 45 mins

This cake is unusual in terms both of look and of taste. It bakes to a deep gold color, the 'honeycomb' effect is fascinating and the distinctive caramel flavor emerges clearly from the dense texture. If you want to make something that is different from the usual run-of-the-mill recipes and the methodology for which is unlike any recipe you have tried before – this is the cake for you! Truly delicious.

1 cup / 200 g granulated sugar
1 cup / 240 ml water
⅓ cup / 80 g butter
6 eggs
⅔ cup / 160 ml condensed milk
1⅔ cups / 215 g all-purpose/ plain flour
2½ tsp baking soda

Heat the oven to 355°F/180°C/Gas Mark 4. Grease a 9-inch/23-cm round cake pan and completely line it with greaseproof paper to ensure that it will hold liquid. Grease again.

1 In a saucepan over a low heat, heat the sugar until it caramelizes into a dark golden brown.
2 Slowly and carefully pour the water into the caramel. The caramelized sugar will spit and steam and reform into lumps. Continue to stir over a low heat until the lumps are dissolved in the water and form a thin syrup. Remove from the heat.
3 Add the butter and allow it to melt in the still-hot syrup. Set aside.
4 In a separate bowl, whisk together the eggs and the condensed milk.
5 Sift the flour and baking soda into the egg and milk mixture and combine well.
6 Add the caramel mixture and mix again.
7 Pour the batter into the prepared cake pan. This is a thin batter so it is important that the cake pan does not leak. Allow the mixture to sit in the pan for five minutes to allow bubbles to develop. Do not tap or knock the pan as this will pop the bubbles.
8 Carefully place the cake in the oven and bake for 45 minutes or until a skewer inserted in the middle comes out clean.
9 Allow the cake to cool in the pan before turning it out onto a plate.

CAMBODIA

Num Taloak

Persimmon Cake

prep 15 mins/bake 25 mins

Persimmons taste like a cross between a plum and an apricot and, provided they are soft and ripe, are delicious. I learned, while searching for persimmons, that Sharon fruits are a cultivar of the persimmon and may be easier to source. Whichever you use it is important that they are over-ripe and squashy, as this is when they are at their sweetest and it will make the flavor of the cake stronger. The recipe will, however, also work with over-ripe peaches, apricots or plums, and is a good way of using up left-over soft fruits.

3 eggs
1½ cups / 300 g caster sugar
½ cup / 115 g butter, melted
¼ tsp salt
2 tsp baking powder
¼ tsp cinnamon
1 tsp vanilla extract
2 cups / 260 g all-purpose/plain flour
¼ cup / 60 ml water
4 ripe persimmons, Sharon fruit or other ripe fruit, peeled, seeded and mashed
1½ cups / 170 g chopped walnuts
2 tbsp confectioner's/icing sugar

Heat the oven to 355°F/180°C/Gas Mark 4.
Grease and lightly flour a 9-inch/22-cm x 11-inch/28-cm cake pan.

1. In a bowl, combine the eggs, sugar and melted butter. Beat until the mixture is light and creamy.
2. Sift the flour, salt, baking powder and cinnamon and fold it into the mixture.
3. Stir in the vanilla extract.
4. Add the mashed persimmon (or other fruit) and chopped walnuts and mix well.
5. Transfer the mixture to the prepared cake pan and bake for 25 minutes or until a skewer inserted in the middle comes out clean.
6. Allow the cake to cool for 10 minutes in the pan, then invert it onto a cooling rack. When the cake is completely cool, sprinkle it with sieved confectioner's/icing sugar.

AFGHANISTAN

Halwaua-e-Aurd-e-Sujee

Halva

Wheat free/Vegan

prep 10 mins/cook 15 mins

Although this mixture is not baked in an oven, I would still class it as a cake, as it is sweet and is served in slices. The combination of scents and tastes in this cake reminded my friends of trips to India and it is true that it is also a popular dessert in northwest India and Pakistan.

1 cup / 200 g granulated sugar
2 cups / 480 ml water
¾ cup / 180 ml ghee
1 cup / 170 g coarse semolina (farina)
¼ cup / 45 g pistachio nuts, blanched
¼ cup / 30 g almonds, blanched
½ tbsp ground cardamom or to taste
1 tbsp rosewater
Nuts for decoration

You will need a heavy, lidded saucepan.
Oil a shallow baking tray.

1. In a saucepan, over a medium heat, combine the sugar and water, stirring until dissolved.
2. Bring the sugar water to the boil for five minutes without stirring.
3. Remove it from the heat and set aside.
4. In a deep, heavy, lidded saucepan melt the ghee over a medium heat and add the semolina. Stir constantly for five minutes, ensuring that the semolina does not scorch or stick.
5. Pour the hot syrup into the semolina, stirring constantly. When it is blended and smooth, reduce the heat and leave the mixture to cook, uncovered, until all the liquid is absorbed. The mixture should be thick but still moist at this stage.
6. Stir in the nuts, cardamom and rosewater.
7. Cover the pan with a cloth or paper towels, put the lid on tightly and leave it on a low heat for five minutes.
8. Remove from the heat and leave the covered pan undisturbed for 10 minutes.
9. Spread the halwau onto the baking tray and decorate it with nuts. Serve the halwaua warm or cold, cutting it into diamond-shaped or square pieces.

JAPAN

Kasutera

prep 20 mins/bake 35-45 mins

Kasutera is a speciality of Nagasaki but the cake is of Portuguese origin and was introduced by traders during the 16th century. The green tea powder gives a subtle effect so if a deeper color is desired add a few drops of green coloring, as I did for the photograph. This cake is rather like a lighter version of a madeira cake in that it is not over-sweet and is delicious eaten buttered. It stores for up to a week in an airtight container. This recipe allows for baking two cakes, one to eat and one to give away. If you only want one, halve the measurements!

- 1 cup / 200 g + 1 tbsp caster sugar
- 7 eggs, separated
- ¼ cup / 60 ml honey
- 1 tsp vanilla extract
- 1 tsp lemon extract
- ¼ tsp salt
- 1⅓ cups / 175 g sieved cake/self-raising flour. Separate the flour into two equal portions and add green tea or cocoa powder to either portion before sieving.
- ⅛ tsp cream of tartar
- 1-2 tbsp green tea powder
- 1-2 tbsp unsweetened cocoa powder

Heat oven to 340°F/170°C/Gas Mark 3.

Use parchment to line the bottom of a two 8-inch/20-cm x 4-inch/10-cm loaf pans. Grease the parchment.

1. Combine the bigger portion of sugar, egg yolks, honey, vanilla extract, lemon extract and salt in a heatproof bowl.
2. Place the bowl over a large pan of simmering but not boiling water. With an electric mixer, beat the mixture for about five minutes on medium-high speed until it turns pale yellow and has doubled in volume. Remove the bowl from the heat.
3. Sift the flour and green tea powder and fold them carefully into the mixture. Set aside.
4. In a separate bowl, beat the egg whites until they are foamy then sprinkle in the tablespoon of sugar and the cream of tartar. Continue beating until the whites are stiff and hold in peaks.
5. Gently fold the egg whites into the cake mixture with a spatula.
6. Divide the mixture equally between the two cake pans. Tap them gently on the worktop to remove any air bubbles.
7. Bake on the middle rack of oven for 35-45 minutes or until golden brown. The cake will pull away from the edges of the baking pan and the top will be flat and feel spongy when pressed with a finger.
8. Cool in the pan for 20 minutes then remove the cake carefully from the pan and gently pull off the parchment. Allow it to cool completely before serving or storing in an airtight container.

PHILIPPINES

Bibingka

Wheat free/Gluten free

prep 10 mins/bake 50 mins

Bibingka is a traditional Christmas treat in the Philippines and was originally wrapped in banana leaves, placed in a terracotta pot and baked over coals. Various toppings of sugar, cheese or grated coconut were then added. It is one of the best coconut cakes I have ever tasted and using grated fresh coconut for the topping, rather than dried, gives a richer flavor.

- 2 cups / 240 g rice flour
- 1 cup / 150 g light brown sugar
- 1 tbsp baking powder
- 3 eggs, beaten
- ⅓ cup / 85 g unsalted butter, melted
- 1⅔ cups / 420 ml coconut milk
- 2 tbsp / 30 g unsalted butter, sliced
- 2 tbsp fresh grated coconut

Grease a round 8-inch/20-cm spring-form cake pan. Heat the oven to 340°F/170°C/Gas Mark 3.

1. Place the rice flour, brown sugar, baking powder, eggs, melted butter and coconut milk in a bowl and mix thoroughly.
2. Pour the batter mixture into the prepared pan and place it on the middle shelf of the oven.
3. Bake for 50 minutes or until golden brown and a skewer inserted in the middle comes out clean.
4. While the cake is still hot, place slices of butter over the surface and then sprinkle with grated fresh coconut.
5. Allow the cake to cool in the pan for 15 minutes before releasing the spring form. Let it cool completely before serving.

TAIWAN

Sweet Potato Cake (see photo overleaf)

prep 50 mins/bake 15 mins

This cake recipe was kindly shown to me by two Taiwanese students who came to stay for a month. We spent a whole evening translating the recipe, which, I like to think, helped their English while providing me with a highly unusual twist on the traditional Swiss roll. Make the filling first so that it is ready to spread on the cake before rolling and do use coloring to counteract the natural but rather dreary look of the sweet potato. It's fair to say that the cake didn't meet with universal acclaim from my colleagues when I brought it into the office but this is a genuine taste of the Far East, with its different dessert traditions.

- 1 lb 7 oz / 600 g white-flesh sweet potato/Eddoes
- 1 tbsp butter
- ¼ cup / 50 g granulated sugar
- 2½ tbsp / 30 g and 5 tbsp / 60 g caster sugar
- 3 oz / 90 g all-purpose/plain flour
- 5 eggs, separated
- 4½ tbsp milk
- ½ tsp salt
- 2 tsp food coloring in the color of your choice
- 1 tsp vanilla extract
- 3 tbsp vegetable oil

Heat oven 340°F/170°C/Gas Mark 3.

Oil a 10-inch/23-cm x 13-inch/33-cm jelly/swiss roll pan then line with greaseproof paper and oil again.

1. Peel the sweet potatoes and cut them into chunks.
2. Steam them until soft.
3. Remove the sweet potato from the heat and mash it until creamy.
4. Divide into two portions of 1 pound 3½ oz / 500g and 3½ oz / 100 g. Set aside the smaller portion.
5. To make the filling, add the butter, white sugar, food coloring, a quarter teaspoon of salt and 2 tablespoons of milk to the larger portion of sweet potato. Combine thoroughly until the filling is an even color. Set aside.
6. Beat together the egg yolks and the smaller amount of caster sugar until light and fluffy.
7. Add the oil and combine thoroughly. Add salt.
8. Sieve the flour into the mixture and combine.

9. Add the smaller portion of mashed sweet potato and gradually add the rest of the milk until thoroughly mixed. Set aside.
10. Whisk the egg whites, gradually adding the rest of the caster sugar, until soft peaks are formed.
11. Add this carefully to the batter, taking care not to over-mix the egg whites.
12. Spread the mixture evenly in the pan and bake for 15 minutes or until golden brown. To test that the cake is cooked, press lightly with your finger: the surface should spring back.
13. While the cake is baking, lay plastic wrap/cling film of the same length as the cake pan on a clean work surface.
14. When the cake is baked, remove it from the oven and tip it out onto the plastic wrap/cling film. Remove the greaseproof paper.
15. Gently press a palette knife into the cake at 1-inch/2.5-cm intervals but take great care not to cut through. This will help to roll the cake. Spread the filling evenly across the cake.
16. Using the plastic wrap/cling film, roll the cake tightly and leave it on a rack to cool thoroughly. Refrigerate until ready to serve.

SRI LANKA

Bibikkan

Wheat free/Gluten free

Coconut Cake (see photo previous page)

prep 30 mins/bake 45 mins

Bibikkan is traditionally made with jaggery, which is a product of sugarcane and the date palm tree. The sugar is unrefined and, when it is cooked, it is set into blocks. It has a rich flavor somewhere between molasses and caramel and is found in Indian and Thai stores. If you can't find it, use dark brown sugar instead. Bibikkan has a delicious warm and spicy flavor and a chewy texture. Once everything is chopped, it is very easy to make and, although it does take a while to bake thoroughly, you will enjoy the delicious smell while you wait.

1½ cups / 225 g jaggery, grated (or dark brown sugar)
1½ cups / 360 ml water
3 cups / 225 g fresh coconut, grated
⅔ cup / 100 g medium semolina flour, roasted
1 cup / 125 g dates, finely chopped
½ tsp fennel seeds, roasted and finely ground
1 cardamom pod, finely ground
¼ tsp cinnamon
3 tsp / 25 g ginger preserve, finely chopped
4 tsp / 25 g candied peel, finely chopped
½ cup / 60 g cashew nuts, finely chopped
¼ tsp salt
½ tsp baking powder
1 egg, separated

Preparation: Heat oven to 320°F/160°C/Gas Mark 3. Generously grease a 13-inch/33-cm x 8-inch/20-cm baking pan.

1. Dry roast the semolina on a baking tray for 10 minutes. At the same time, roast the fennel seeds on a heatproof plate for 10 minutes.
2. In a saucepan, over a medium heat, dissolve the grated jaggery (or brown sugar) in water.
3. Add the coconut and cook for 2-3 minutes. Remove from the heat and set aside to cool.
4. Crush the fennel seeds and seeds from the cardamom pod in a pestle and mortar until you have a fine powder.
5. When the jaggery mixture is cool, stir in the semolina, dates, fennel and cardamom powder, ginger preserve, candied peel, cashew nuts, salt, baking powder and cinnamon.
6. Beat the egg yolk and add to the mixture.
7. Beat the egg white until soft peaks are formed and fold in carefully, taking care not to over-mix.
8. Pour the batter into the greased baking pan and bake for 45 minutes or until a skewer inserted in the middle comes out clean.
9. Allow to cool in the pan for 10 minutes before inverting onto a cooling rack. Cut into squares when completely cool.

CHINA

Nian Gao

New Year Cake

prep 15 mins/cook 50 mins

Wheat free/Vegan

Nian Gao is also known as Sticky Cake. It is made as part of the Chinese New Year celebrations and is traditionally an offering to the Chinese Kitchen God. It is well named as it is sticky and chewy, and so is best served in thin slices. I added a mix of dried fruits that included cranberries and apricots to give the finished cake some color, but you can also add nuts and dates. The mixture should be steamed in a wok or a traditional steamer.

- 3¼ cups / 400 g glutinous rice flour
- 1 cup / 130 g brown sugar or 2 slabs (about 5 oz / 140 g) Chinese brown candy (peen tong in Cantonese; pian tang in Mandarin)
- ¾ cup + 2 tbsp / 200 ml boiling water
- ½ cup dates, chopped and softened in water, or ½ cup other dried fruit
- 1 tbsp milk
- Water, as needed
- 1 tbsp white sesame seeds

Oil a 7-inch/17.5-cm cake pan.

1. In a bowl, pour the boiling water over the sugar and stir until dissolved. If using peen tong/pian tang, break the candy into several pieces, so that it will dissolve more easily in the boiling water. Set aside to cool.
2. Place the glutinous rice flour in a large bowl. Make a well in the middle and stir in the sugar and water mixture. Add the milk.
3. Begin shaping the dough, incorporating two-thirds of the dried fruit as the dough is worked. If the mixture is dry, gradually add a tablespoon of water at a time, until the dough becomes smooth.
4. Put the dough into the greased cake pan and spread it out to the edges. Decorate with the remaining dried fruits by lightly pushing them into the surface of the cake. Finish by sprinkling with the sesame seeds.
5. Place the cake tin in the wok or steamer over medium-high to high heat for 50 minutes. Try to resist lifting the lid to check the cake as the heat will be lost and the cake will take longer to cook through. After 50 minutes remove the cake from the heat and cool.
6. Use a knife to loosen the edges and invert the cake onto a plate to cool. Wrap in greaseproof paper and refrigerate overnight.
7. To serve, cut the cake into quarters, and then into thin slices. Nian Gao can be served cold or reheated in the microwave for 10-15 seconds. It can also be dipped in an egg wash and pan fried in a little oil.

CAKE LIST

Caribbean & North America

RECIPES FROM...

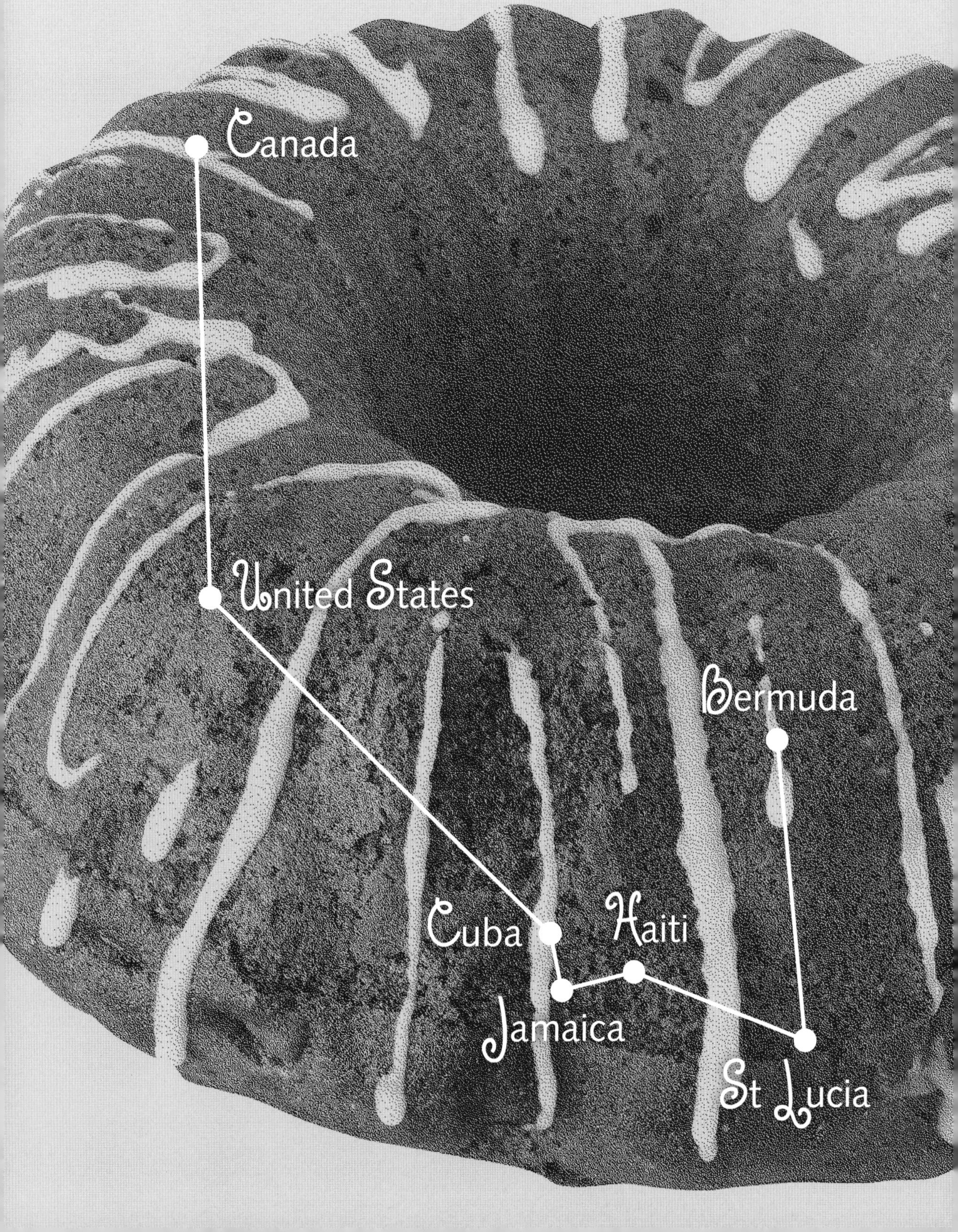

Canada

United States

Bermuda

Cuba

Haiti

Jamaica

St Lucia

UNITED STATES

Red Velvet Cake (see photo overleaf)

prep 45 mins/bake 25 mins

This is a celebration cake that never fails to impress and has a real wow effect. It is difficult to make a truly red cake, which is why I have included beetroot in the coloring paste. You might try using gel rather than liquid for the food coloring because it will result in a deeper red. Do use a high-quality cocoa powder as this will also help the color of the cake. The addition of white chocolate makes the cream-cheese frosting really special while also providing an intense contrast to the red sponge.

1 cup / 250 g butter, softened
3 cups / 600 g caster sugar
6 eggs
4 tbsp red food coloring
4 tbsp best-quality cocoa powder
¼ cup / 50 g cooked beetroot
3½ cups / 450 g all-purpose/ plain flour
1 cup / 240 ml buttermilk
1 tsp vanilla extract
½ tsp salt
1 tsp baking powder
1 tsp bicarbonate of soda
2 tsp white vinegar

Frosting

1⅔ cups / 400 g cream cheese
3½ cups / 350 g white chocolate, broken into squares
1 cup / 250 g butter, softened

Heat the oven to 340°F/170°C/Gas Mark 3.

Grease three 8-inch/20-cm cake pans. Line with greaseproof paper and grease again.

Cake

1. In a large bowl, cream the butter and sugar until light and fluffy.
2. Add the eggs one at a time, beating well after each addition.
3. In a separate bowl, mix the food coloring with the cocoa and mashed beetroot to make a paste. Add to the mixture, combining well until the color is even.
4. Sieve the flour, salt and baking powder together. Add this to the mixture one-third at a time, alternating with one-third of the buttermilk, until all the flour and buttermilk are absorbed.
5. Add vanilla extract.
6. In a small bowl, mix bicarbonate of soda with vinegar – expect them to 'fizz' slightly when combined. Whisk while adding to the cake mix, then stir thoroughly. (The addition of the vinegar and bicarbonate develops the color of the cake while it is baking).

7 Divide the mixture equally between the three prepared pans and place in the oven for 25 minutes or until a skewer inserted in the middle comes out clean.
8 Allow the cakes to cool for 5 minutes before removing them from the pans. Allow them to cool thoroughly then refrigerate – preferably overnight, but for at least 4 hours.

Frosting

1 Melt the white chocolate in a bowl over just boiling water, taking care not to allow the water to come into contact with the base of the bowl. Allow the chocolate to cool to lukewarm.
2 In a large bowl, beat the cream cheese until light and fluffy.
3 Gradually beat in melted white chocolate and softened butter.
4 Continue to beat the icing until it has the consistency of whipped cream.
5 Spread over each layer and then cover the whole cake.

CANADA

Maple Syrup Cake

(see photo previous page)

prep 30 mins/bake 35 mins

This is an easy celebration cake to make for grown-up birthdays. The butter icing is really smooth and creamy while the chopped pecans make for a pleasing crunchy contrast. If you can find maple extract, add 2 teaspoons to the cake and 1 teaspoon to the icing for an even more intense flavor, but it is just as good without.

2 eggs, beaten
2 cups / 260g all-purpose/plain flour
¾ cup / 180 ml maple syrup
½ cup / 100 g butter
½ cup / 100 g caster sugar
½ cup / 70 g chopped pecans
¾ cup / 180 ml buttermilk
2½ tsp baking powder
½ tsp ground ginger
1 tsp vanilla extract
½ tsp salt

Frosting
1¼ cups / 285 g butter, softened
6 cups / 650 g confectioner's/icing sugar, sieved
⅔ cup / 150 ml whipping cream
⅓ cup / 75 ml maple syrup
Whole pecans to decorate

Heat the oven to 355°F/180°C/Gas Mark 4.

Grease sides of two 9-inch/23-cm round metal cake pans. Line the base with parchment or waxed paper and lightly grease again.

Cake

1. In a large bowl, beat together the eggs, maple syrup, butter, sugar and vanilla until light and fluffy (about 5 minutes). Set aside.
2. In a separate bowl, sieve together flour, baking powder, ginger and salt. Set aside.
3. In a jug, mix the buttermilk and maple syrup.
4. Alternately add the dry ingredients and buttermilk liquid to the creamed egg mixture, making 3 additions of dry ingredients and 2 of the liquid. Beat well after each addition.
5. Stir in the chopped pecans.
6. Divide the mixture between the prepared pans, making an indentation in the center of each to ensure a flatter surface when the cake has baked.
7. Bake in the center of the oven for about 35 minutes or until a skewer inserted in the middle comes out clean.
8. Let the cakes cool in their pans on a rack for 10 minutes. Turn out onto the rack, peel off the greaseproof paper and allow them to cool completely.

Frosting

1. Beat the butter until light and fluffy.
2. Alternately beat in the confectioner's/icing sugar and cream, making 3 additions of sugar and 2 of cream.
3. Add the maple syrup and maple extract (if you have it).
4. Trim the top of cakes to level if necessary. Spread a generous amount of butter icing on one cake and top with the other.
5. Cover the cake with the remaining butter icing and decorate with the whole pecans.

HAITI

Gâteau au Beurre

prep 25 mins/bake 50 mins

This is a very moist, and (not surprisingly, given the title) buttery cake that is good to eat on its own with a cup of coffee or to serve as a dessert with fruit and cream. I baked it in a silicone mold and was very pleased with the result: the cake had a shiny glaze and took on the shape of the mold really well, picking out the detail in sharp relief. The decoration made a plain cake look special. Please note that, if you do not have a pan of the recommended size, this recipe needs quite a big one.

- 2 cups / 300 g softened butter
- 2 cups / 400 g caster sugar
- 6-8 eggs, separated
- 4 cups / 520 g all-purpose/plain flour
- 2 tsp baking powder
- ¼ tsp salt
- 1 cup / 240 ml milk
- 1 tbsp pure vanilla extract
- 1 tbsp rum
- ½ tsp lemon zest

Grease and flour a 10½-inch / 27-cm square cake pan.
Heat the oven to 355°F/180°C/Gas Mark 4.

1. Cream the butter, gradually adding the sugar, and beating until light and fluffy.
2. Beat the egg yolks in a bowl then gradually add to the butter and sugar mixture, beating well after each addition. Set aside.
3. In a bowl, sift the flour, salt and baking powder together.
4. Alternately add one-third of the sifted dry ingredients and half of the milk to the creamed mixture so that you start and finish with the dry ingredients.
5. Stir in the vanilla extract, rum and lemon zest and combine thoroughly. Set aside.
6. In a clean, dry bowl, whip the egg whites until they form soft peaks.
7. Carefully fold the beaten egg whites into the batter, taking care not to over-mix.
8. Pour the mixture into the prepared cake pan.
9. Bake for 50 minutes or until a skewer inserted in the middle comes out clean.
10. Let the cake cool in the pan a few minutes, then turn it out onto a wire rack to cool completely.

ST LUCIA

Banana Cake

(see photo overleaf)

prep 10 mins/bake 35 mins/decorate 20 mins

This would make a great birthday cake for a banana fan. The combination of spices and tropical fruit is mouth watering. The cream-cheese frosting, topped with caramelized bananas, gives it a cheesecake texture, with a final added crunch from the walnuts – wonderful! Do take care when browning the banana slices, as they burn very easily. This was a great favorite in the office.

2½ cups / 350 g cake/self-raising flour
1 tsp bicarbonate of soda
2 tsp mixed spice
1 cup / 150 g light brown sugar
4 large eggs
¾ cup + 1 tbsp / 200 ml sunflower oil
2 bananas, mashed
½ cup / 100 g fresh pineapple, finely chopped
Zest and juice of 1 orange
⅔ cup /100 g walnuts, roughly chopped

Frosting
1⅔ cups / 400 g medium-fat cream cheese
3 tbsp / 50 g butter, softened
1½ cups / 200 g confectioner's/icing sugar, sieved

Caramelized bananas
3 medium bananas
2 tbsp caster sugar
½ tsp lemon juice

Grease and flour two 8-inch/20-cm cake pans.
Heat the oven to 355°F/180°C/Gas Mark 4.

1. In a large bowl, sift the flour, bicarbonate of soda and mixed spice.
2. Add the sugar and combine well. Set aside.
3. In a separate bowl, whisk the eggs and the oil until smooth.
4. Gradually add the egg and oil mixture to the flour mixture, stirring all the while until completely combined.
5. Add the mashed bananas, pineapple, orange zest and juice and chopped walnuts. Stir well.
6. Divide the mixture equally between the pans and bake for 35 minutes or until the top is golden brown and a skewer inserted in the middle comes out clean.
7. Allow the layers to cool in the pans for 10 minutes then remove them to a cooling rack and allow them to cool completely.

Frosting

1. In a bowl, beat together the soft cheese and butter until completely combined.
2. Gradually add the confectioner's/icing sugar until the mixture is smooth and creamy.
3. Spread half of the frosting over one layer, cut one banana into thin slices and arrange over the frosting and place the other layer on top. Cover with the remaining frosting.

Caramelized bananas

1. Line a baking tray with greased foil or greaseproof paper.
2. Combine the lemon juice and sugar in a bowl.
3. Cut 2 bananas into thin slices into the mixture and ensure the slices are covered.
4. Using a palette knife to pick up the slices, arrange on the baking tray.
5. Grill on a low to medium heat for 2-3 minutes or until the banana slices are browned.
6. Allow them to cool for 10 minutes, then lift and arrange on the cake.

BERMUDA

Rum Cake (see photo previous page)

prep 35 mins/bake 40 mins

This cake has a good strong flavor and a wonderful spicy aroma. It's advisable to weigh everything out before you start and be aware that you will need at least 3 separate bowls for combining the ingredients. It is well worth the effort but be warned that the clue is in the title – this is a very rummy cake!

2 cups / 260 g strong wholewheat flour (or spelt flour)
2 tsp baking powder
1 tsp baking soda
1 cup / 150 g dates, chopped
⅔ cup / 100 g brazil nuts, chopped
1½ cups / 250 g pineapple, chopped and drained
2 large eggs
½ tsp ground black pepper
¼ tsp ground cloves
½ tsp cinnamon
1¾ cups + 1 heaped tbsp / 225 g muscovado sugar
½ cup / 125 ml corn oil

Topping
½ cup / 100 g caster sugar
¼ cup / 50 ml water
2 separate measures of 2½ fl oz / 75ml and 3⅓ fl oz / 100ml of dark rum

Glacé icing
2 tbsp confectioner's/icing sugar, sieved
1-2 tsp water

Heat the oven to 355°F/180°C/Gas Mark 4.
Butter a deep, 8-inch/20-cm ring pan.

1. In a bowl, combine the flour with the baking powder and soda.
2. In a separate bowl, combine the dates and nuts with the pineapple.
3. Break the eggs into a large bowl and set aside.
4. Warm the spices, pepper and muscovado sugar in a saucepan over a low heat.
5. Add the warmed sugar mixture to the eggs and beat with an electric mixer for 3-4 minutes, until light and fluffy.
6. Add the oil and the smaller measure of rum, then the flour mixture. Beat until smooth.
7. Stir in the nuts, pineapple and dates, then spoon into the prepared pan.
8. Bake for 40 minutes, until risen and firm to the touch.
9. While the cake is baking: boil the caster sugar with the water in a saucepan, then remove from the heat and allow to cool before adding the remaining bigger measure of rum. Set aside.
10. When the cake is baked, remove it from the oven and spoon half of the syrup over while it is still in the pan, then leave for 30 minutes.
11. After 30 minutes, gently ease the cake away from the pan sides with a knife, invert onto a plate and spoon the remaining syrup over the top.
12. When the cake is completely cooled, make a small amount of glacé icing to drizzle over the top. Add water to the confectioner's/icing sugar until a drizzling consistency is reached. The white icing offers a great contrast to the dark cake.

JAMAICA

Ginger Cake with Lemon Glacé Icing

prep 20 mins/bake 50 mins

Ginger cakes should be moist to the point of stickiness and this is no exception. Don't worry if the batter seems a bit runny as this is what results in such a lovely moist cake. However, there is a danger of the cake sinking when it cools so just invert the cake on a cooling rack when it comes out of the oven. If necessary, use the base as the top and your secret will be safe!

- 1¾ cups / 225 g all-purpose/plain flour
- 2 tsp baking powder
- ½ tsp bicarbonate of soda
- 1 tsp ground allspice
- ½ tsp grated nutmeg
- 2 tsp ground ginger
- 1 cup / 225 g unsalted butter
- ¾ cup / 125 g light brown sugar
- ⅓ cup / 85 g drained stem ginger, grated
- ½ cup / 120 ml evaporated milk
- ½ cup / 120 ml black treacle (or molasses)
- 2 eggs

Icing

- ½ cup / 75 g confectioner's/icing sugar
- Zest and juice of 1 lemon

Heat the oven to 355°F/180°C/Gas Mark 4.

Grease a 10½-inch/27-cm x 6-inch/15-cm loaf pan. Line with greaseproof paper and grease again.

1. In a large bowl, sift the flour, baking powder, bicarbonate of soda, allspice nutmeg and ground ginger.
2. Add the butter and beat until well combined.
3. Add the sugar and the grated ginger. Mix well. Set aside.
4. In a saucepan and on a low heat mix together the evaporated milk and black treacle. Heat and stir gently until the two ingredients have combined, making sure the mixture does not bubble. The liquids will combine quite suddenly so will need close supervision.
5. Once the treacle and milk have combined, remove from the heat and pour into the batter. Stir until thoroughly mixed.
6. Beat in the eggs.
7. Pour the batter into the pan and bake for 50 minutes or until a skewer inserted in the middle comes out clean.
8. Leave to cool in the pan for at least 30 minutes, as ginger cakes are particularly fragile on coming out of the oven. Remove from the pan and allow to cool thoroughly.
9. Mix together the confectioner's/icing sugar, lemon zest and lemon juice, adding water if required. The icing should have a thick, glossy consistency that will ooze over the cold cake but not run off. Spoon over the loaf as desired.

CUBA

Opera Cake (see photo overleaf)

prep 90 mins/bake 35 mins

Our photographer (and official taster) described this as 'a box of chocolates in a cake'. It's simpler than the French version, which has seven layers, but is still a rich and satisfying experience. Coffee and chocolate complement each other so well and this is the cake that expresses that fusion perfectly. For chocolate lovers everywhere.

130 g dark chocolate, chopped
2 cups / 260 g all-purpose/plain flour
2 tsp baking soda
½ tsp salt
1½ cups / 225 g light brown sugar
½ cup / 115 g unsalted butter at room temperature
3½ tsp vanilla extract
4 large eggs
1 cup / 240 ml sour cream
½ cup / 120 ml crème de cacao
½ cup / 120 ml freshly brewed coffee, lukewarm

Buttercream

1½ cups / 235 g chocolate, chopped
½ cup / 65 g confectioner's/icing sugar
4 large egg yolks
2 tbsp water
2 tbsp corn syrup/golden syrup
½ cup / 115 g and ¼ cup / 80 g unsalted butter, room temperature

Coffee mousse

½ cup / 120 ml mixed heavy/double cream and milk (also known as 'half and half')
4 tbsp caster sugar
1 tbsp instant espresso or coffee powder
4 large egg yolks
1 tsp unflavored gelatin softened in 1 tablespoon water for 10 minutes or 1 tsp of agar powder, which is suitable for vegetarians/vegans and will have the same gelling effect.
1 cup / 240 ml chilled whipping cream
1 tsp vanilla extract

Chocolate glaze

1½ cups / 300 g caster sugar
1 cup / 240 ml water
½ cup / 50 g unsweetened cocoa powder
1¾ cup / 340 g dark chocolate, chopped

Heat the oven to 340°F/170°C/Gas Mark 3.

Grease with butter two 9-inch/23-cm cake pans with sides that are 2 inches/5 cm deep. Line the bottoms with parchment paper rounds and grease again. Dust the pans with flour; tap out the excess.

1. In a heatproof bowl or in the top of a double boiler, melt the chopped chocolate over simmering water, stirring until melted and smooth. Remove from the heat and allow to cool until it is lukewarm.
2. In a separate bowl, combine flour, baking soda, and salt. Set aside.
3. In a large bowl, beat sugar, butter, and vanilla until creamy.
4. Add the eggs one at a time to the creamed mixture, beating well into the mixture after each addition.
5. Gradually add the lukewarm melted chocolate, ensuring it is well combined.
6. Add the dry ingredients to the mixture one-third at a time, alternating with half of the sour cream so that you start and finish with the dry ingredients.
7. Gradually add the crème de cacao and coffee, beating well after each addition.
8. Divide the batter evenly between the prepared pans, taking care to smooth the tops with a palette knife.
9. Place in the oven and bake for 35 minutes or until a skewer inserted in the middle comes out clean.
10. Leave cakes to cool in the pans on a rack for 10 minutes, then invert onto 9-inch/23-cm cardboard rounds or a removable tart pan bottom. Allow to cool completely.

Buttercream

1. In a heat-proof bowl or in the top of a double boiler, melt the chopped milk chocolate, stirring until melted and smooth. Set aside to cool to lukewarm.
2. In a metal or heat-proof bowl, whisk together the sugar, egg yolks, 2 tablespoons of water, and the corn/golden syrup until they are thoroughly combined.
3. Add 1/4 cup / 80 g butter.
4. Place the bowl over a saucepan of simmering water; whisk constantly for about 4 minutes.
5. Remove the bowl from the saucepan and beat the mixture until it is completely cool and thick.
6. Beat in 1/2 cup / 115 g of butter, about 1 tablespoon at a time, ensuring each addition is thoroughly mixed.
7. Beat in the lukewarm melted chocolate.

Coffee mousse

1. In a medium bowl, whisk the egg yolks and 2 tablespoons of the sugar until well blended.
2. In a saucepan over a medium to high heat, simmer the milk and cream mixture, 2 tablespoons of the sugar, and the espresso powder. Remove when the mixture starts to bubble slightly.
3. Gradually whisk the hot coffee liquid into the egg mixture.
4. Return the mixture to the saucepan and stir constantly over a low to medium heat for about 2 minutes. Pour into a large bowl.
5. Add the gelatine/agar; stir until dissolved then beat well until cool. Set aside.
6. In a medium bowl, beat the whipping cream and vanilla until stiff peaks form. Fold into the coffee mixture.

To assemble

1. Cut each cake layer horizontally in half. Trim the top of the cakes to level if necessary.
2. Place one cake layer in the bottom of a 9-inch/23-cm spring-form pan. Cover with half of the buttercream.
3. Place the second cake layer on top of the buttercream and cover with mousse.
4. Top with the third layer of cake. Refrigerate for up to 1 hour to allow mousse to set.
5. When the mousse is set, spread the remaining half of buttercream over the third layer. Top with the fourth cake layer (the cake will rise above the rim of the pan). Cover with film and refrigerate for at least 4 hours or overnight.

Chocolate glaze

1. In a saucepan, over a medium heat, stir the sugar and water until the sugar dissolves.
2. Increase the heat and bring to the boil.
3. Whisk in the cocoa until combined then remove from the heat.
4. Add the chocolate and whisk until the chocolate has melted and the mixture is smooth. Let the glaze cool but keep checking that it is still pourable. This will take up to 1 hour.
5. Run a knife around the pan sides to loosen the cake and release it from the tin. Scrape any excess mousse from the sides of the cake.
6. Carefully transfer the cake onto the plate on which it will be presented. Pour the glaze over the cake, spreading it with a spatula until the whole cake is covered.
7. Refrigerate for at least 2 hours to allow the glaze to set. Let the cake stand at room temperature for 1 hour before serving.

CAKE LIST

Oceania & Pacific

RECIPES FROM...

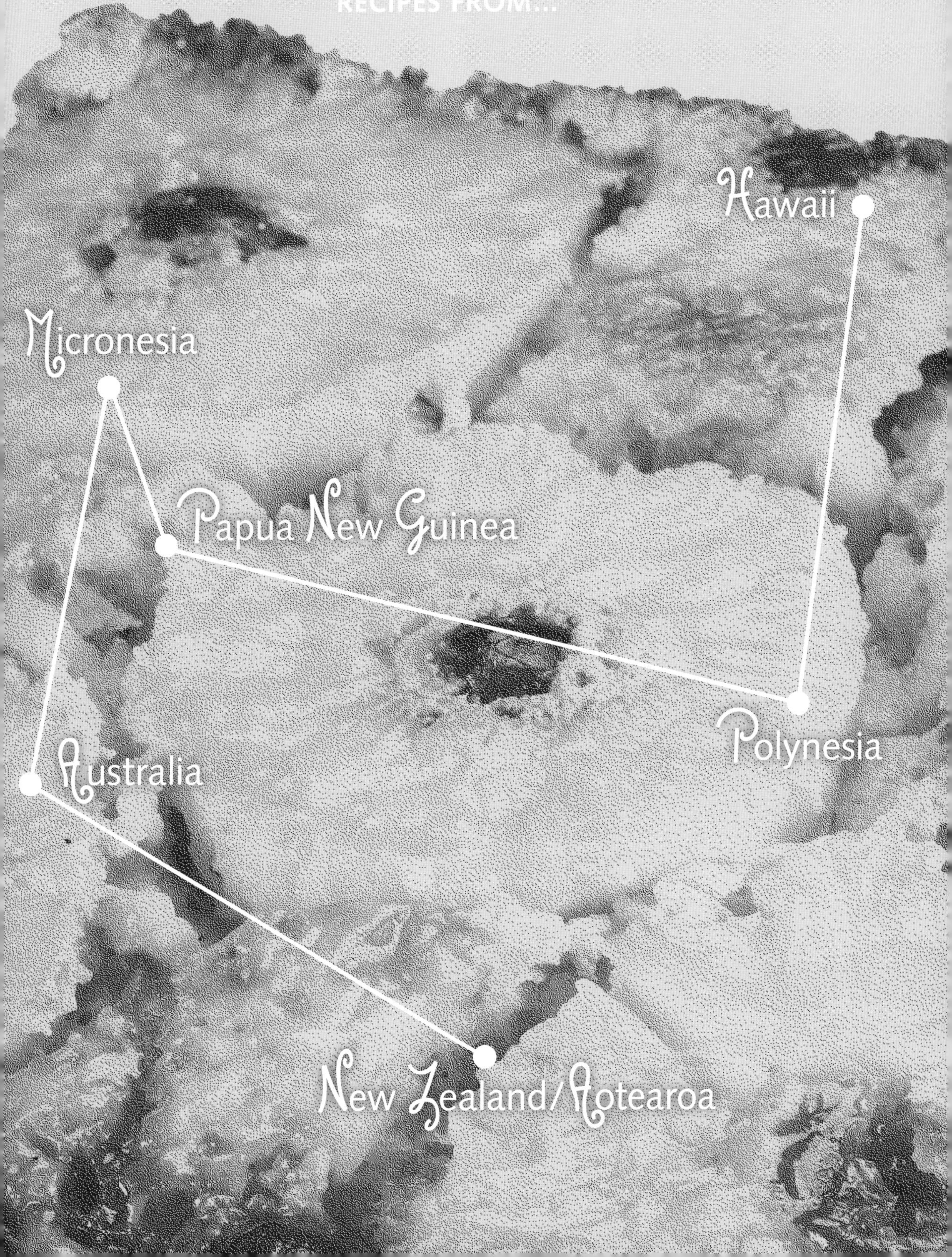

Hawaii

Micronesia

Papua New Guinea

Polynesia

Australia

New Zealand/Aotearoa

MICRONESIA

Glazed Orange Coconut Cake

prep 20 mins/bake 35-40 mins

This is such a gorgeous, moist cake that it can be eaten unadorned – but why not make it even more special with this orangey glaze, decorated with toasted coconut? Brown the flakes under a medium grill but take care, as they can burn very easily. Please note the cake is soft so you will need to drizzle the glaze and then spread it with care.

2½ cups / 325 g all-purpose/plain flour
1½ cups / 300 g caster sugar
¾ cup / 70 g finely shredded, fresh coconut
½ teaspoon salt
2 tsp baking powder
2 tsp baking soda
1 cup / 240 ml coconut milk
½ cup / 120 ml vegetable oil
2 eggs
1 tsp vanilla extract
1 cup / 240 ml freshly squeezed orange juice
1 tbsp freshly grated orange zest

Glaze

2 cups / 270 g confectioner's/icing sugar
¼ cup / 60 ml fresh orange juice (about 1 orange)
Toasted desiccated coconut and orange zest to decorate

Grease or oil a large bundt pan (round with a hole in the middle).

Heat the oven to 355°F/180°C/Gas Mark 4.

1. In a large bowl, combine the flour, sugar, shredded coconut, salt, baking powder and baking soda. Set aside.
2. In a separate bowl, combine the coconut milk, vegetable oil, eggs, vanilla, orange juice and zest and thoroughly mix together.
3. Add the wet ingredients to the dry and mix until smooth and creamy.
4. Pour the mixture into the prepared pan and bake for 35-40 minutes, or until a skewer inserted in the middle comes out clean.
5. Allow the cake to cool completely in the pan before removing it to a cooling rack. The cake must be cold before adding the glaze.
6. For the glaze, sieve the icing sugar into a bowl.
7. Slowly add the orange juice and combine together until the mixture reaches a consistency that spreads over the cake easily.
8. Sprinkle with the toasted coconut and orange zest.

PAPUA NEW GUINEA

Banana Cake with Chocolate Sauce

prep 35 mins/bake 40-50 mins

Bananas, cocoa and coconuts are all crops grown in Papua New Guinea and they taste like a dream when mixed together and baked in this cake. Although the taste is fabulous, the cake looks quite plain so I used a decorative bundt tin to make it look a bit more interesting. If you put the chocolate sauce in a ramekin in the middle, everyone can help themselves. The cake is best served while still warm and covered with the chocolate sauce.

- ½ cup / 115 g butter, softened
- ½ cup / 100 g caster sugar
- 1 tsp vanilla extract
- 2 eggs, beaten
- 2 medium-size bananas, mashed
- 1 tsp baking soda
- 1½ cups / 195 g all-purpose/plain flour
- 1½ tsp baking powder
- ½ cup / 120 ml whole milk

Sauce

- ¾ cup / 135 g dark chocolate chips
- ½ cup / 120 ml coconut milk

Pre-heat oven to 355°F/180°C/Gas Mark 4. Grease and lightly flour a 9-inch/23-cm bundt pan (round with a hole in the middle).

1. In a large bowl, mix the butter, sugar and vanilla extract until the mixture is pale and creamy.
2. Gradually add the beaten eggs and mashed bananas, beating well after each addition. Set aside.
3. In a separate bowl, sift the flour, baking soda and baking powder.
4. Gradually add the milk until a thick batter is formed – do not make it too runny, especially if you are using over-ripe bananas. Add to the banana mixture and combine well.
5. Pour into the cake pan and bake for 40-50 minutes or until a skewer inserted in the middle comes out clean.
6. Remove the cake from the oven and allow it to stand for 10 minutes before turning it out onto a cooling rack.
7. To make the sauce, place the chocolate chips in a heatproof bowl.
8. Heat the coconut milk in a saucepan until it is just boiling, stirring intermittently to prevent scorching.
9. When the milk is just bubbling, pour it over the chocolate, ensuring the chips are completely covered.
10. After the sauce has cooled for about 10 minutes and looks melted, gently stir, then beat until smooth.

AUSTRALIA

Pineapple Upside Down Cake

prep 20 mins/bake 30 mins

Using fresh pineapple for the topping makes for a paler finish but intensifies the flavor throughout. The cake has a soft, fruity texture and can be served hot as a dessert with custard or cream or cold with ice cream. It keeps well when refrigerated although I can't imagine that you will need to store it for long!

- 1½ cups / 200 g all-purpose/ plain flour
- ½ tsp salt
- ½ cup / 100 g caster sugar
- 2 tsp baking powder
- 3 medium eggs, separated
- ½ tsp vanilla extract
- ¾ cup / 190 ml unsweetened pineapple juice
- ½ cup / 100 g butter, melted

Glaze and topping

- ⅓ cup / 75 g butter, melted
- ¾ cup /175g soft dark brown sugar
- 1 small fresh pineapple, peeled, cored and cut into rings
- Glacé cherries (optional)

Heat the oven to 375°F/190°C/ Gas Mark 5.

Grease an 11-inch/28-cm x 9-inch/23-cm high-sided baking pan.

Glaze and topping

1. In a bowl, combine the melted butter with the dark brown sugar and 4 tablespoons of the pineapple juice.
2. Pour the mixture over the base of the prepared pan, making sure it is completely covered.
3. Arrange the pineapple rings and cherries on top of the mixture in a decorative pattern. Set aside.

Cake

1. Combine the flour, salt, caster sugar and baking powder. Set aside.
2. In a separate bowl, beat the egg yolks until pale and creamy. Stir in the vanilla, the remaining pineapple juice and melted butter.
3. Add the egg mixture into the dry ingredients until just combined. Set aside.
4. In a separate bowl, beat the egg whites until they form stiff peaks. Gently fold into the cake mixture, taking care not to over-stir.
5. Pour the batter evenly over the top of the pineapple rings.
6. Bake for 30 minutes or until a skewer inserted in the middle comes out clean.
7. Let the cake cool for 10-15 minutes then, after easing around the edge of the cake with a palette knife, cover the pan tightly with a serving dish and invert it so that the cake is tipped out, pineapple side up.

Louise Cake

prep 20 mins/bake 20-25 mins

This is one of those cakes that is simple to make but that everyone loves. The ingredients can be found in most store cupboards, although if you can add some fresh raspberries they will add a bit of sharpness to balance the jam, as well as providing color to the meringue topping. It is easy to see why the Louise Cake has been a favorite in New Zealand/Aotearoa for so many years.

- ½ cup / 125 g butter, at room temperature
- ¾ cup / 150 g caster sugar
- 3 large eggs, separated
- 2½ cups / 325 g all-purpose/plain flour
- 2 tsp of baking powder
- ½ tsp of vanilla extract
- ¾ cup / 200 g raspberry jam

Topping

- 3 egg whites (from the separated eggs)
- ¼ cup / 50 g caster sugar
- 1¼ cups / 120 g unsweetened, desiccated coconut
- 1 tsp vanilla extract
- A handful of fresh raspberries, if available

Heat oven to 300°F/150°C/Gas Mark 2.

Lightly grease an 11-inch/28-cm x 8-inch/20-cm cake pan. Line the pan with baking paper and allow the paper to hang over the edges a little.

1. In a mixing bowl, cream together the butter and sugar until light and fluffy.
2. Add the egg yolks, one at a time, beating well after each addition. Add the vanilla extract.
3. Sift the flour and baking powder then fold into the mixture until combined. This will result in a crumbly dough.
4. Press the dough into the lined cake pan until the base is covered and then completely cover it with a thin layer of jam (you can also sprinkle the jam with some fresh raspberries if you have them). Set aside while you make the topping.
5. In a separate bowl, beat the egg whites until they form soft peaks.
6. Gradually add the caster sugar, one tablespoon at a time, while continuing to beat the whites until they form stiff, glossy peaks.
7. Using a spatula, gently fold in the desiccated coconut and vanilla extract.
8. Spread the coconut meringue over the jam, ensuring that the jam is completely covered.
9. Bake in the oven for 20-25 minutes or until the meringue has developed a lightly golden brown and soft pink color. It is quite normal for it to crack.
10. Remove the cake from the oven and allow it to cool in the pan for 10 minutes. Lift it from the tin and onto a cooling rack, using the lining paper, and allow it to cool completely.
11. Once the cake has cooled, cut it into squares and serve topped with fresh raspberries (if available). The cake can be kept in an airtight container for up to one week.

POLYNESIA

Wedding/Carrot Cake

(see photo overleaf)

prep 40 mins/bake 50 mins

This cake has been described as a wedding cake but actually it's a really good carrot-cake recipe – and every baking book worth its salt should include a carrot cake. It has a moist, 'chunky' texture, while using fresh pineapple and coconut gives it a delicious tropical flavor. While carrots are not a crop that springs to mind when you are thinking of Polynesian islands, they are actually grown in this region of the South Pacific all year round.

2½ cups / 325 g all-purpose/plain flour
2 tsp cinnamon
2 tsp baking soda
1 tsp salt
1 cup / 225 g mashed pineapple, drained
1 cup / 240 ml vegetable oil
3 eggs
2 cups / 400 g caster sugar
2 cups / 180 g finely shredded carrots
1 cup / 125 g chopped nuts
¾ cup / 50 g finely shredded coconut
1 cup / 150 g chopped dates (optional) or 1 cup / 150 g raisins (optional)

Frosting

½ cup / 100 g cream cheese, softened
1 tbsp milk
½ tsp vanilla extract
¼ cup / 50 g butter, softened
1 cup / 85 g toasted coconut
3 cups / 400 g confectioner's/icing sugar

Heat the oven to 355°F/180°C/Gas Mark 4.

Grease a 13-inch/33-cm x 9-inch/23-cm baking pan and set aside.

1 In a large mixing bowl, using a wooden spoon throughout (do not use a mixer), combine the oil and sugar until blended.
2 Add the eggs, one at a time, mixing well after each addition and ensuring the batter is smooth. Add the vanilla.
3 Gradually add the flour, cinnamon, baking soda and salt, stirring well, and ensuring the batter is smooth after each addition. Keep a spatula close by to clean the sides of the bowl. Once all these dry ingredients are incorporated, this will result in a stiff batter.
4 Add the shredded carrots, chopped nuts, pineapple and coconut and mix just until combined.
5 Pour the mixture into the pan and bake for 50 minutes or until golden brown and a skewer inserted in the middle comes out clean. Allow the cake to cool in the pan for 10 minutes then cool completely on a rack.

Frosting

1 In a bowl, cream together the cream cheese and butter.
2 Add the confectioner's/icing sugar, milk, vanilla extract and toasted coconut, keeping a little coconut back for decoration if desired.
3 When the cake is completely cool, spread the frosting on top.
4 Decorate with toasted coconut.

HAWAII

Guava Chiffon Cake (see photo previous page)

prep 40 mins/bake 35-40 mins

Guava does not have a strong flavor but this chiffon cake allows its fruity taste to come through. You will need a light touch when folding the mix into the egg whites so that the finished cake does not lose its 'light as air' texture. Remember not to grease the pans, otherwise the mixture will not be able to rise as it should.

2¼ cups / 290 g cake/self-raising flour
1 tbsp baking powder
1 tsp salt
¾ cup / 150 g and ½ cup / 100 g granulated sugar
½ cup /120 ml vegetable oil
1 cup / 240 ml guava juice
5 egg yolks, lightly beaten
2 to 3 drops red food coloring (optional)
8 egg whites, room temperature
½ tsp cream of tartar

Topping

1 tbsp corn starch/cornflour
2 tbsp water
1¼ cups / 300 ml guava juice

Frosting

1½ cups / 360 ml heavy/double cream
⅓ cup / 45 g confectioner's/icing sugar
½ cup / 120 ml guava juice

Preheat oven to 340°F/170°C/Gas Mark 3. Cover wire cooling racks with plastic wrap. Use two 9-inch/23-cm cake pans of the deeper kind. Do not grease or oil them.

1. In a large bowl, sieve together the flour, baking powder, and salt.
2. Add the larger of the two quantities of sugar and combine well.
3. Add the vegetable oil, guava juice, beaten egg yolks, and food coloring (if desired). Whisk for one to two minutes, or until the mixture is smooth. Set aside.
4. In a large bowl, beat the egg whites and cream of tartar until soft peaks form.
5. Add the rest of the sugar, a tablespoon at a time, continuing to beat until stiff peaks form.
6. Using a spatula, carefully fold a third of the cake mixture into the egg-white mixture until just barely mixed. Gently fold in the remaining cake mixture, taking great care not to over-mix.
7. Pour the mixture into the ungreased cake pans, smoothing the surface with a palette knife when they are full.
8. Bake for 35-40 minutes or until a skewer inserted in the middle comes out clean.
9. Remove from the oven and invert the cakes onto the prepared wire rack. When the cakes have cooled completely, they should be gently removed from the pans and refrigerated until required.

Topping

NB Only prepare the topping when you are ready to complete the cake.

1 In a small bowl, combine the corn starch and water until the starch is dissolved.
2 In a small saucepan and over a medium-high heat, bring the guava juice to the boil, then reduce heat instantly.
3 Add the corn-starch mixture and stir until it thickens to a sauce-like consistency.
4 Remove from the heat and let the topping cool to lukewarm.

Frosting

1 In a large bowl, beat the cream until soft peaks form.
2 Gradually add the sugar, continuing to beat until stiff peaks form.
3 Add the guava juice, ensuring it is combined well.
4 Refrigerate until you are ready to ice the cake.

Assembly

1 When the cake is well chilled, remove it from the refrigerator. Place one cake layer on a plate and spread it with half the lukewarm guava topping. Top with the remaining cake layer.

NB To keep the cake from sliding to one side, insert a long wooden skewer into the middle and all the way to the bottom.

2 Spread the remaining guava topping on top of the cake. Smooth with a palette knife.
3 Use the frosting to decorate the sides and top of the cake.
4 Store in the refrigerator until serving time.

CAKE LIST

Latin America

RECIPES FROM...

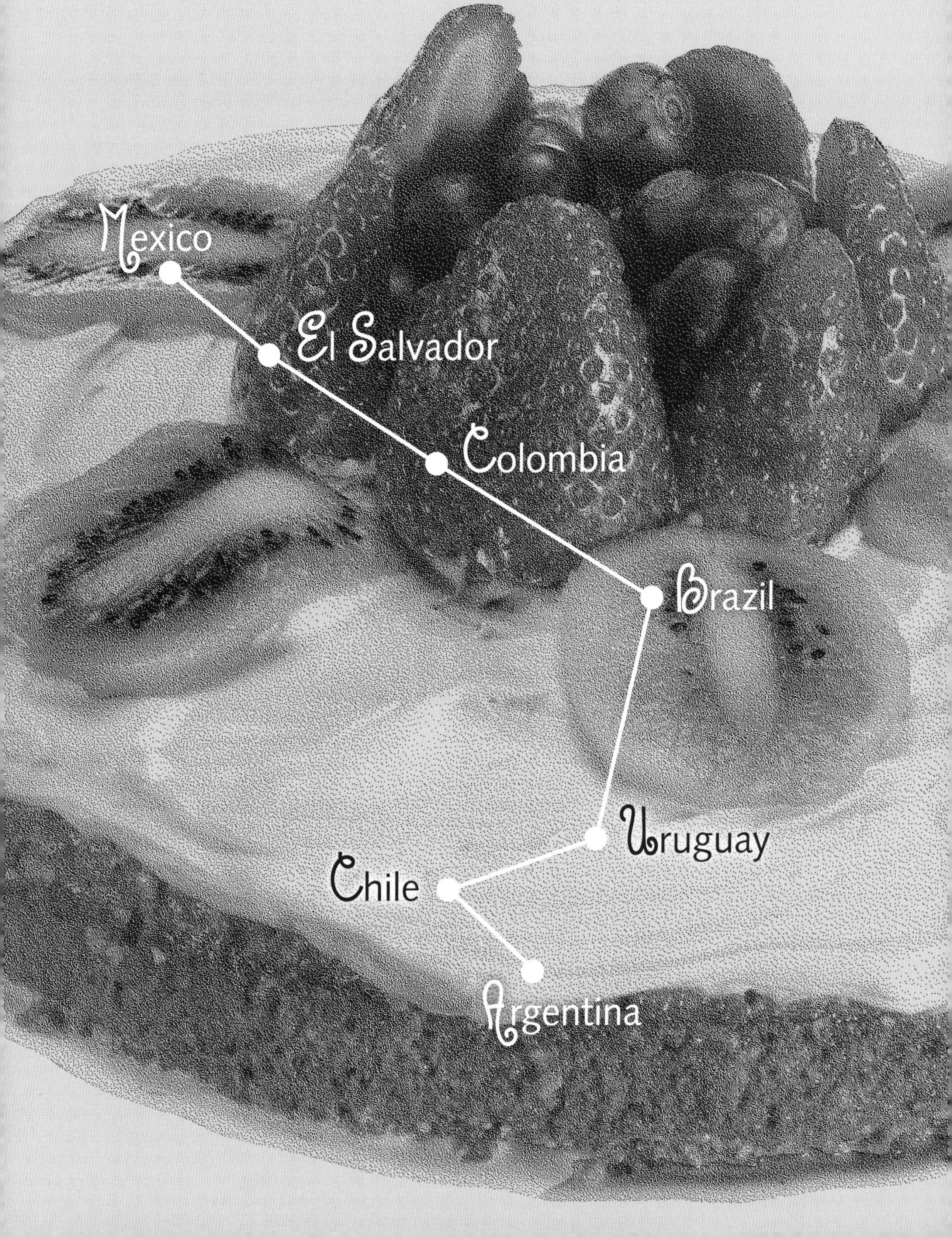

Mexico

El Salvador

Colombia

Brazil

Uruguay

Chile

Argentina

CHILE

Torta de Hojas

prep 20 mins (filling 3 hours)/bake 50 mins/assemble 30 mins

Friends and family cannot fail to be impressed by this 'Cake of Leaves'. The filling soaks into the layers of sweet pastry, forming a cake that, when sliced, gives the impression of being made up of many more layers than the 10 'leaves'. The sweetness of the caramel is balanced by the warmth of the brandy.

- 4 cups / 520 g all-purpose/plain flour
- 2 tsp baking powder
- 3 egg yolks
- 1 cup / 225 g butter
- 1½ cup / 360 ml milk

Ingredients for the filling

- 2 x 14 oz / 400 g cans condensed milk
- 1 cup / 225 g chopped walnuts + whole walnuts to decorate
- ¼ cup / 60 ml brandy
- ¼ cup / 60 ml water

Heat oven to 355ºF/180ºC/Gas Mark 4.
Oil two baking sheets, cover with greaseproof paper and oil again.

Caramel

1. Place the unopened cans of sweetened condensed milk in a saucepan and cover with water.
2. Boil for 3 hours. Take great care to ensure the cans are always covered by water as they will explode if the pan is allowed to boil dry.
3. Remove the cans from heat and let them cool for 15 minutes before opening.

Cake

1. Mix together the flour and baking powder and set aside.
2. In a large bowl, beat the butter until creamy.
3. Blend in the egg yolks, one at a time.
4. Add the flour mixture alternately with the milk, adding the milk gradually to form a stiff but not sticky, dough.
5. Divide the dough into 10 equal pieces and shape into balls. Roll each ball into a 9-inch/23-cm circle.
6. Place the pastry circles on baking sheets and prick with a fork all over to prevent the pastry from bubbling.
7. Bake for 10 to 12 minutes, or until golden brown.
8. Transfer the leaves onto a cooling rack and continue in this way until all 10 leaves are baked and cooled.
9. In a small measuring cup, combine the brandy and water.
10. When the caramel is ready, place one pastry layer on a serving plate, sprinkle with brandy mixture, then spread with the caramel sauce. Sprinkle with the chopped walnuts. Continue stacking in this way, adding the sauce and chopped walnuts until all the layers have been stacked, but keeping back enough caramel mixture to go on top.
11. Once you have put the caramel mixture on the top, decorate with the whole walnuts.
12. Allow the cake to soak up the filling for at least two hours, and preferably overnight, before cutting.

BRAZIL

Cuca de Banana

prep 40 mins/bake 50 mins

Although there are three cakes in this book that include banana as one of the main ingredients, each of them is very different. This delicious recipe has a crunchy seam running through the middle that contrasts with the soft texture of the main mixture. It is delicious whether served warm with cream or cold with a cup of Brazilian coffee.

5 ripe bananas
4 eggs, separated
2 cups / 400 g caster sugar
¾ cup / 180 ml vegetable oil
1 cup / 240 ml buttermilk
1 tsp vanilla extract
4 cups / 520 g all-purpose/plain flour
1 tbsp baking powder
1 tsp salt

Crumb topping/filling

½ cup / 65 g all-purpose/plain flour
¼ cup / 50 g granulated sugar
¼ cup / 40 g light brown sugar
1 tsp cinnamon
¼ tsp salt
1¾ oz / 50 g cold butter

Preheat the oven to 355°F/180°C/Gas Mark 4. Using butter, grease the sides of a 9- or 10-inch/20- or 23-cm spring-form pan. Line the bottom of the pan with a circle of wax paper then grease again.

Crumb topping/filling

1 Mix the flour, sugars, cinnamon and salt in a small bowl.
2 Cut the cold butter into small pieces and add to the flour mixture.
3 Mix the butter into the flour and sugar with your fingers, rubbing the butter and dry ingredients together until the mixture is well blended and forms large crumbs. Refrigerate until required.

Cake

1. Peel and slice the bananas into ¼-inch/1-cm slices and set aside.
2. In a bowl, beat the egg yolks and the sugar until pale and fluffy.
3. Add the vegetable oil, buttermilk, and vanilla extract and mix well.
4. In a separate bowl, stir the baking powder and salt into the flour, then gradually add the flour mixture to the cream mixture. Note that the flour should be just mixed into the batter and not beaten or over-stirred. Set aside.
5. In a clean, dry bowl, beat the egg whites until they are stiff enough to form peaks, then gently fold into the batter with a spatula taking care, once again, not to beat or over-stir the mixture.
6. Pour half of the mixture into the prepared cake tin.
7. Layer half of the banana slices on top of the batter, then sprinkle about half of the crumb mixture over them.
8. Spread the remaining batter on top of the first layer, then cover it with the remaining banana slices and sprinkle the rest of the crumb mixture over the top.
9. Bake for 40-50 minutes or until the crumb mixture on top is golden brown or until a skewer inserted in the middle of the cake comes out clean. If the top looks baked and the middle is still undercooked, lower the heat of the oven to 340°F/170°C/Gas Mark 3 and continue until it is baked through.
10. Remove the cake and cool it in the tin on a rack for 15 minutes before liberating it from the pan. Serve warm or at room temperature.
11. The cake can be stored in the refrigerator for up to one week.

MEXICO

Pastel de Tres Leches

Three Milks Cake

prep 35 mins/bake 30-40 mins

'Pastel de Tres Leches' is a speciality of Latin American countries and derives its name from the three milks used in the soaking sauce – condensed milk, evaporated milk and heavy/double cream. Not surprisingly, this is an extremely dense and moist cake, rather like sliceable custard. That means it is certainly not an everyday cake but one to bake for pure indulgence on a special occasion.

- 1½ cups / 195 g cake/self-raising flour
- 1 tsp baking powder
- ¼ tsp salt
- ⅓ cup / 80 ml oil
- 1 cup / 200 g caster sugar
- 1 tsp vanilla extract
- 5 large eggs
- ½ cup / 120 ml whole milk

Sauce

- 12 oz / 340 g evaporated milk
- 14 oz / 400 g sweetened condensed milk
- ½ cup / 120 ml heavy/double cream
- 1 tbsp rum or brandy (optional)

Topping

- ¾ cup / 180 ml heavy/double cream
- 1 tsp vanilla extract
- 1 tbsp confectioner's/icing sugar
- Cinnamon or fruit of choice for decoration (optional)

Lightly grease a 9-inch/23-cm spring-form cake pan.
Heat the oven to 340°F/170°C/Gas Mark 3.

1. In a bowl, combine the flour, baking powder and salt.
2. In a separate bowl, combine the oil, sugar, and the vanilla extract.
3. Add the eggs, one at a time, to the sugar mixture, beating well after each addition.
4. Stir in the milk.
5. Gradually fold the sugar mixture into the flour mixture.
6. Pour batter into the cake pan and bake for 30-40 minutes or until a skewer inserted in the middle comes out clean.

7 Let the cake cool in the pan for 30 minutes then carefully turn it out onto a serving plate with a raised edge. The raised edge is important as the sauce will initially run out of the cake and will need to be contained so it can be spooned over the cake.
8 Pierce the cake with a fork 20-30 times then allow it cool in the refrigerator for at least another 30 minutes.

Sauce

1 Whisk together the three milks and the rum or brandy.
2 Slowly pour the liquid over the cooled cake.
3 Refrigerate for at least one hour but during this time keep going back and spooning the excess sauce back onto the surface of the cake. Keep doing this until the cake has absorbed the sauce.

Topping

1 In a chilled mixing bowl, add heavy cream, vanilla and sugar and beat well until peaks form.
2 When the cake has absorbed all the sauce, spread the topping over it.
3 Decorate with a sprinkle of cinnamon or garnish with fruit if so desired.

EL SALVADOR

Quesadilla Salvadoreña

Salvadoran Sweet Cheese Pound Cake

prep 20 min/Bake 25 min

Part of the fun of creating this book has been using ingredients I wouldn't normally dream of including in a cake recipe. Who would have thought that hard cheese would taste so good in a sweet cake? *Quesadilla* is a rich, sweet dessert cake often found in local *panaderías* (bakeries) in El Salvador. They traditionally contain unsalted Salvadoran *queso fresco*, a fresh farm cheese, but parmesan cheese or a vegetarian hard-cheese equivalent can be used instead. At first my tasters were skeptical, but they demolished the whole cake in one sitting!

- 1 cup / 130 g all-purpose/plain flour
- 1 tsp baking powder
- 2 cups / 145 g finely grated hard cheese
- 1 cup / 200 g caster sugar
- 2 eggs, beaten
- ¼ cup / 60 ml sour cream and ¼ cup / 60 ml whole milk combined
- ½ cup / 115 g butter, melted
- 1 tsp sesame seeds

Heat oven to 355°F/180°C/Gas Mark 4.
Grease a 5-inch/12.5-cm x 9-inch/23-cm loaf pan.

1. Sift the flour and baking powder together into a bowl.
2. In a bowl, beat together the grated cheese (keeping a little aside for decorating the cake), sugar, eggs and sour cream/milk mixture until creamy.
3. Stir in the melted butter.
4. Slowly add the sifted flour mixture until fully combined and the batter is smooth.
5. Pour the batter into the loaf tin.
6. Sprinkle on sesame seeds and the last of the grated cheese.
7. Bake for 20 to 25 minutes, or until a skewer inserted in the middle of the cake comes out clean.
8. Remove the cake from the oven and allow it to cool completely before slicing and serving.

COLOMBIA

Spiced Coffee Sponge Cake

prep 20 mins/bake 25 mins/frost/ice 15 mins

(see photo overleaf)

This is by far the best coffee cake I have ever tasted – it is adapted from a recipe by the National Federation of Coffee Growers of Colombia. It looks quite ordinary until you bite into the explosion of spices and coffee in the sponge and frosting. The smell while it is baking is just heavenly. I used a clean tea towel to strain the coffee and milk and it worked very efficiently. The frosting is really a rich and creamy coffee custard. Irresistible!

4 tbsp /30 g ground 100% Colombian coffee
¾ cup / 180 ml milk
1½ cups / 195 g all-purpose/plain flour
1 tsp baking powder
½ tsp salt
½ tsp cinnamon
½ tsp nutmeg
¼ tsp ground cloves
3 eggs
1 cup / 200 g caster sugar
1 tsp vanilla extract
¼ cup warm melted butter

Frosting
½ cup brewed hot 100% Colombian coffee
⅓ cup / 65 g caster sugar
Pinch salt
3 egg yolks
1 cup / 240 g butter, softened
1 tsp vanilla extract

Grease and flour 2 x 8-inch/20-cm round cake pans.
Heat the oven to 355°F/180°C/Gas Mark 4.

1. Combine the coffee and milk in a saucepan and bring to a boil, then allow the liquid to stand on a low heat for 10 minutes.
2. Strain the mixture through cheesecloth or a clean tea towel into a small bowl. Return the coffee-flavored milk to the saucepan and keep it warm over low heat.
3. In a bowl, sift the flour, baking powder, salt, cinnamon, nutmeg and cloves. Set aside.
4. In a large bowl, beat eggs until they thicken.

5. Slowly add the sugar, continuing to beat well after each addition.
6. Add the coffee-flavored milk and vanilla, stirring until just blended.
7. Fold the flour and spices into the mixture until just blended, taking care not to overbeat.
8. Fold the melted butter in carefully.
9. Pour the batter into the pans. Bake for 20-25 minutes or until a skewer inserted in the middle comes out clean.
10. Allow the sponges to cool for 10 minutes, then turn them out onto racks so they can cool completely.
11. To make the frosting, combine the coffee, sugar, salt and egg yolks in a heat-proof bowl.
12. Over simmering water, beat the ingredients until the mixture has thickened.
13. Remove from the heat and continue to beat until the mixture has cooled.
14. Add the butter one tablespoon at a time, beating well after each addition.
15. Add the vanilla and continue to beat until the mixture is thick enough to spread.
16. When the cake has completely cooled, spread the frosting over one layer and place the other layer on top. Cover the cake with the remaining frosting.

ARGENTINA

Torta Negra Galesa

Black Welsh Cake (see photo previous page)

prep **12** hours/bake **1** hour

In 1865, 150 Welsh people settled in the Chubut Valley, in the Argentine region of Patagonia, in an attempt to protect their language and culture. The settlers survived by peaceful co-operation with the native peoples and today Welsh is still taught and spoken in that part of Argentina. I like the fusion between the two cultures evident in this recipe, which mixes more familiar ingredients with rum, molasses and spices. Please don't be put off by the preparation time for this cake as for most of that time the fruit and nuts are soaking in the rum while you go about your business! The cake has a delicious, rich flavor that improves the longer it is kept.

1 cup / 225 g butter, softened
1¼ cup / 165 g soft dark brown sugar
5 eggs, separated
2 tbsp molasses/black treacle
3 tbsp honey
2½ cups / 325 g all-purpose/plain flour
1 tsp allspice
2 tsp cinnamon
2 tsp baking powder
1 cup / 140 g roughly chopped walnuts, almonds, or hazelnuts, or a mix of all three
½ cup / 80 g raisins
½ cup / 80 g sultanas
½ cup chopped candied fruit peel
¼ cup chopped maraschino or glacé cherries
1 cup rum

Decoration

1½ cups / 200 g confectioner's/icing sugar
3-4 tbsp fresh orange juice
Chopped nuts and raisins

Soak the nuts, raisins, and candied fruit in the rum overnight. Drain the nuts and fruit and reserve the rum.

Heat the oven to 340°F/170°C/Gas Mark 3.

1. Cream the butter with the brown sugar.
2. Gradually beat in the egg yolks, molasses/black treacle and honey.
3. Sift the flour with the cinnamon, allspice, and baking powder into the batter and mix until combined.
4. Stir in nuts, raisins, fruit and reserved rum. Set aside.
5. In a separate bowl, beat the egg whites until they form stiff peaks. Fold the egg whites gently into the batter, taking care not to over-mix.
6. Pour the batter into an 8-inch/20-cm square cake pan.
7. Bake for 45 minutes or until a skewer inserted in the middle comes out clean.

Decoration

1. In a bowl, sift the confectioner's/icing sugar.
2. Add the orange juice 1 tablespoon at a time, until a slightly runny consistency is reached.
3. Spread the icing over the top of the cake, and sprinkle with raisins and nuts.

URUGUAY

Postre Chajá

Peach Cake

prep 2 hrs 50 mins/bake 60 mins

This is quite an undertaking to make from scratch but it results in a wonderfully light and frothy confection that looks and tastes quite different from other celebration cakes. Invented by a famous confectioner, Orlando Castellano, it is named after a large South American bird called *el chajá*, also known as a 'crested screamer'. This large bird has air pockets beneath its feathers that reduce its weight, inspiring Castellano to create the cake. If you want to save time, you can use ready-made meringue for the filling and decoration.

2 cups / 260 g sifted all-purpose/plain flour
1½ cups / 300 g caster sugar
1 tbsp baking powder
1 tsp salt
½ cup /120 ml vegetable oil
7 eggs, separated
¾ cup / 180 ml cold water
2 tsp vanilla extract
2-3 tsp grated lemon or orange peel
½ tsp cream of tartar

Meringue
4 egg whites
½ tsp cream of tartar
1 cup / 200 g caster sugar
¼ tsp salt
½ tsp vanilla extract

Peaches and peach syrup
6 or 7 peaches
1 cup / 200 g caster sugar
1 cup / 240 ml water
1 tsp vanilla extract
2 tbsp rum or peach-flavored vodka (optional)

Frosting
2 cups / 480 ml heavy/double cream
2 tbsp sugar
½ tsp vanilla extract
Pinch of salt

(recipe continues overleaf)

Postre Chajá

Peach cake

Heat the oven to 390°F/200°C/Gas Mark 6. Use two ungreased 9-inch/23-cm cake pans.

Meringue

1 Beat the egg whites and cream of tartar until stiff peaks start to form.

2 Gradually add the sugar and continue to beat until peaks are very stiff and the sugar is dissolved.

3 Beat in the vanilla and a pinch of salt.

4 Cover a baking sheet with parchment paper. Fill a piping bag with the egg-white mixture and pipe small dollops of meringue onto the parchment. Alternatively, pipe the meringue in strips that can be crumbled once they are cooked and used to decorate the outside of the cake.

5 Bake for at least 1½ hours or until the meringues are dry and crisp. When completely cool, store in an airtight container until required.

Cake

1 Reduce the heat of the oven to 340°F/170°C/Gas Mark 3.

2 In a large mixing bowl, sift together the flour, sugar, baking powder, and salt.

3 Make a well in the middle of the sifted dry ingredients and add the oil, egg yolks, water, vanilla, and lemon or orange peel. Beat well until the mixture is smooth. Set aside.

4 In a large mixing bowl, beat the egg whites with the cream of tartar until very stiff peaks form.

5 Pour the creamed egg-yolk mixture over the whipped egg whites, gently folding in with a rubber spatula just until blended. Do not stir or beat.

6 Pour the batter into the ungreased cake pans.

7 Bake for 50 minutes, then increase the heat to 355°F/180°C/Gas Mark 4 and continue baking for 10 minutes.

8 Remove the cake from the oven and invert the pans so that they hang without the cakes touching a surface e.g. between two pans or racks. Allowing them to cool in this way will ensure that the rise is retained.

9 Once the cake has cooled, loosen the sides gently with a spatula and remove the cakes from the pans.

Peaches and peach syrup

1. Peel and slice peaches into a strainer over a bowl.
2. Cover the peach slices with 1-2 tablespoons of sugar and allow to drain for 20 minutes. Set aside the juice.
3. Bring the water, sugar and reserved peach juice to a boil, and simmer until the sugar is dissolved. Remove from the heat and allow it to cool.
4. Stir in vanilla extract, pinch of salt, and rum or vodka (optional). Set aside.

Frosting

1. In a bowl, combine the sugar and cream and whip until medium stiff peaks are formed.
2. Stir the vanilla into the whipped cream, and refrigerate until required.

To assemble

1. Turn the sponge cakes upside down and liberally spoon over the peach syrup until both cakes are soaked.
2. Place one cake right side up on a serving platter. Cover with whipped cream then crumble some meringue pieces over the cream.
3. Arrange a generous layer of peach slices over the meringue and cream, reserving some slices to decorate the top of the cake, then top with the second cake layer.
4. Spread whipped cream around the sides and top of cake.
5. Press meringue circles or crumbs into the cream on the sides of the cake.
6. Decorate the top with the remaining peach slices and pieces of meringue.
7. Chill thoroughly before serving.

CAKE LIST

Eastern Europe & Central Asia

RECIPES FROM...

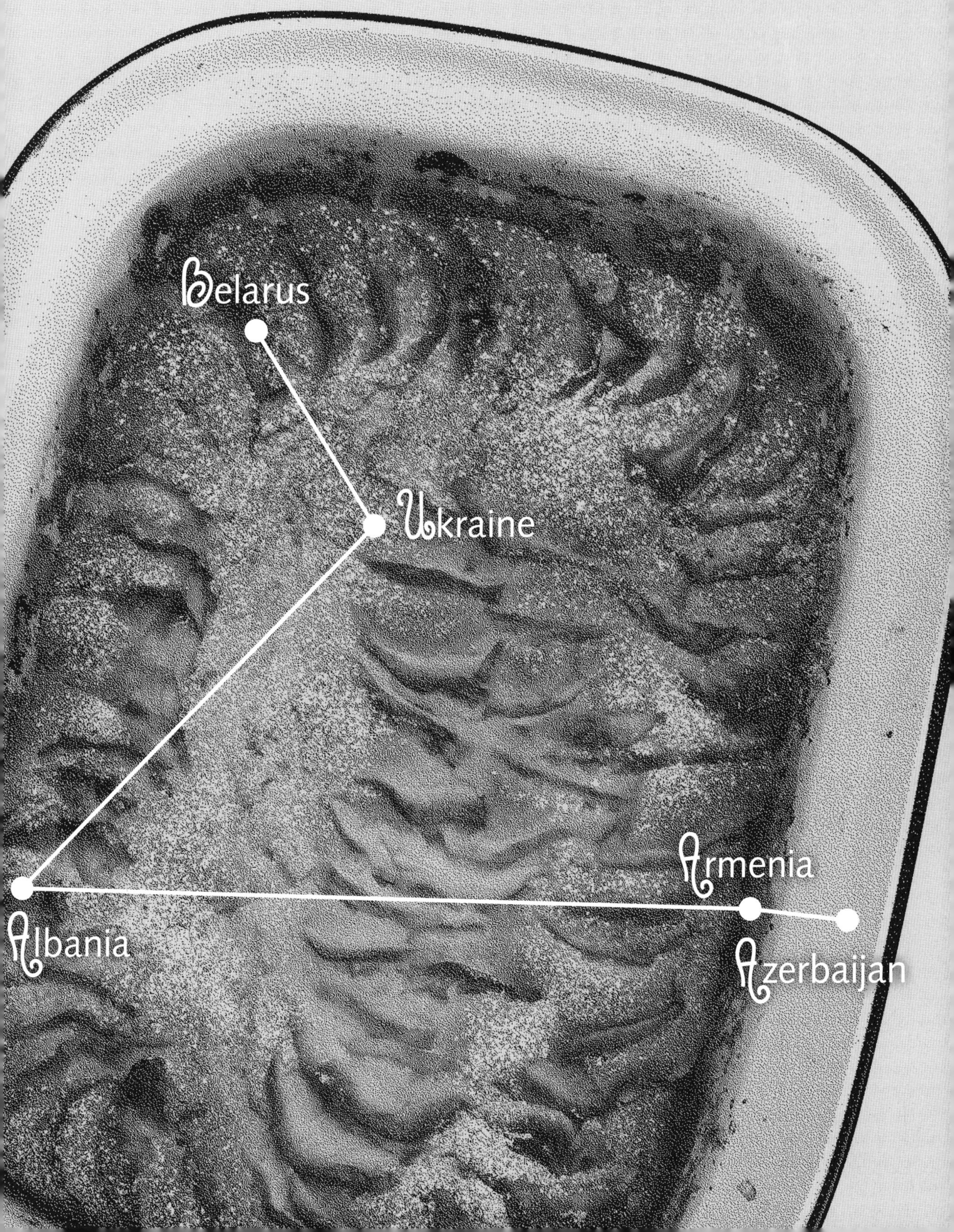

Belarus

Ukraine

Armenia

Albania

Azerbaijan

BELARUS

Yablochny Pirog

Apple Torte

prep 15 mins/bake 40 mins

This simple little cake can be whipped up in minutes and is equally delicious whether served hot as a pudding with custard or served cold as a cake. The layer of apples cooked through the middle and the addition of sour cream make for a really moist texture and the sponge has a shortbread quality. This is a great way of using up that glut of apples in the autumn.

2 eggs
1 cup / 200 g caster sugar
1 cup / 130 g all-purpose/plain flour
½ cup / 115 g butter
½ cup / 65 g corn starch/cornflour
1½ tsp baking powder
½ tsp vanilla extract
3 tbsp sour cream
4 cooking apples, peeled and thinly sliced
A little confectioner's/icing sugar for sifting on top of the finished torte

Grease and flour an 8-inch/20-cm spring-form cake pan – though a deep pie dish will do, so long as it is well greased.

Heat the oven to 375°F/190°C/Gas Mark 5.

1. Place all the ingredients, except for the apples, in a large bowl and combine well until a thick batter is formed.
2. Pour half the batter into the cake pan and spread two-thirds of the apple slices evenly on top of the batter, then pour remaining batter over the apples.
3. Arrange the remaining slices in a pattern on the top of the cake.
4. Bake for 40 minutes.
5. Allow the torte to cool for 10 minutes before releasing the sides of the pan and turning the torte out onto a cooling rack.
6. When the torte is completely cold, sift confectioner's/icing sugar on top.

ALBANIA

Walnut Cake with Lemon Glaze

prep 30 mins/bake 40 mins

This is a spicy cake that is difficult to resist while you are waiting for it to cool! The lemon glaze is delicious and the spices smell wonderful. It keeps well, and the flavor is even better after a day or two.

½ cup / 115 g butter, softened
¾ cup / 150 g caster sugar
2 eggs, lightly beaten
⅓ cup / 80 ml plain yogurt
⅓ cup / 80 ml buttermilk
2 cups / 260 g all-purpose/ plain flour
1 tsp baking powder
1 tsp baking soda
½ tsp cinnamon
1 tbsp lemon rind finely grated
1 cup /115 g walnuts, toasted and finely chopped

Glaze

¾ cup / 180 ml water
1 cup / 200 g caster sugar
½ tsp ground cinnamon
¼ cup / 60 ml fresh lemon juice
¼ tsp ground allspice
¼ tsp ground cloves

Heat the oven to 355°F/180°C/Gas Mark 4.
Butter a 9-inch/23-cm x 13-inch/32.5-cm baking pan.

1. Cream together the butter and sugar until light and fluffy.
2. Gradually add the beaten eggs, beating well in between each addition.
3. In a jug, blend the yogurt with the buttermilk.
4. In a separate bowl, sift the dry ingredients together. Add half of this to the butter/sugar/egg mixture, followed by the yogurt mixture and then the other half of the dry ingredients, blending thoroughly with each addition.
5. Stir in the lemon rind and chopped walnuts.
6. Pour the cake mix into the greased baking pan and bake for 30 minutes or until a skewer inserted in the middle comes out almost clean. Note that the cake should still be slightly undercooked when covered with the glaze.
7. While the cake is baking, put all the ingredients for the glaze into a saucepan over a medium heat, cover and simmer for about 15 minutes. Remove from the heat.
8. When the cake is almost done, remove it from the oven and turn the oven off.
9. Pour the glaze over the hot cake and return it to the still-hot oven for about 10 minutes.

ARMENIA

Nutmeg Cake

prep 10 mins/bake 40 mins

This cake is so simple to make but results in a real mixture of tastes and textures. It is unusual to use the same mixture both for the base and the top but this works really well, with the nuts turning it into something like a crunchy cake sandwich. The cake has a dark and spicy taste and it simply flew off the plate when I brought it into the office.

- 2 cups / 260 g all-purpose/ plain flour, sifted
- 1 tsp baking powder
- 1 pinch salt
- ½ cup / 100 g cold butter, roughly chopped
- 2 cups / 260 g soft dark brown sugar
- 1 tsp baking soda
- 1 cup / 240 ml milk (or sour cream)
- 1 egg, lightly beaten
- 1 tsp ground nutmeg
- ½ cup / 60 g walnuts or ½ cup / 60 g pecans, chopped

Grease a 9-inch/23-cm square pan, and line with baking paper if desired.

Heat the oven to 355°F/180°C/Gas Mark 4.

1. In a large bowl, combine the flour, baking powder and salt.
2. Rub in the butter until the mixture resembles fine breadcrumbs.
3. Add the sugar and combine well.
4. Divide the mixture in half and press half of the mixture evenly over the base of the prepared cake pan.
5. In a separate bowl, mix the baking soda into the milk (or sour cream).
6. Add the beaten egg and nutmeg.
7. Add the milk and egg mixture to the remaining flour mixture and combine together well.
8. Pour over the base in the cake pan and sprinkle with the chopped nuts.
9. Bake in the oven for 40 minutes or until a skewer inserted in the middle comes out clean.
10. Allow the cake to stand for 10-15 minutes before turning onto a wire rack to cool.

AZERBAIJAN

Zebra Cake

prep 25 mins/bake 40 mins

This simple cake looks very impressive despite not using frosting/icing or bright coloring. The patterns on the top and throughout, made by the alternate rings of cake mix, are really beautiful – they take the concept of a marble cake to another level. Feathering the top results in a delicate cobweb pattern, which means this would be a great cake to make for Hallowe'en.

4 large eggs, at room temperature
1¼ cups / 250 g granulated sugar
1 cup / 240 ml milk, at room temperature
1 cup / 240 ml oil (corn, vegetable or canola are fine)
1 tsp vanilla extract
2⅓ cups / 300 g all-purpose/plain flour
3 tsp baking powder or 1 tsp baking soda
2 tbsp dark cocoa powder

Heat the oven to 355°F/180°C/Gas Mark 4. Grease a 9-inch/23-cm round cake pan with oil. Line with parchment paper and oil again. You will need a large serving spoon or a ladle.

1. In a large mixing bowl, whisk the eggs and sugar until the mixture is pale and creamy.
2. Add the milk, oil and vanilla extract and continue beating until well blended. Set aside.
3. In a separate bowl, combine the flour and baking powder. Gradually add the flour mixture to the wet ingredients, beating after each addition until the batter is smooth but taking care not to overbeat in order to prevent air pockets from forming in the mixture.
4. Divide the mixture into two equal portions. Leaving one portion plain, sieve the cocoa powder into the other portion and mix until it is thoroughly combined and not streaky.
5. Using the large spoon or ladle, scoop a spoonful of plain batter into the middle of the pan. Then place an equal-sized scoop of the cocoa batter in the middle of the plain batter. Continue to alternate between the different colors in this way, always placing each portion in the middle of the pan. Do not wait for the batter to spread between each addition, do not attempt to spread the batter yourself or tilt the pan. The mixture will spread by itself and will fill the pan gradually. Continue adding alternate and equal measures of the mixtures until both batters are used up.
6. The top can be 'feathered' at this stage. Lightly drag a skewer through the surface of the mixture from the middle of the cake to the edge. Each time, lift the skewer out of the mixture and go back to the middle of the cake, dragging in one direction only and being careful to pull the skewer lightly along the surface. Do this five or six times evenly around the cake.
7. Carefully place the cake in the oven and bake for 40 minutes. Do not open the oven door for at least 25 minutes as this cake is prone to collapsing. Don't be too concerned if cracks appear on the top of the cake as it bakes, since the cracks close as the cake cools. The cake is ready when a skewer inserted in the middle comes out clean.
8. Remove from the oven. Immediately run a knife around the inside of the pan to loosen the cake, then invert the cake onto a cooling rack.

UKRAINE

Medivnyk

Christmas Honey Cake

prep 25 mins/bake 60 mins

This cake is traditionally made at Christmas in Ukraine but is also produced for other celebrations such as the Jewish festival of Rosh Hashanah. The honey and dark sugar give it a rich taste while the coffee brings out the flavors of the fruit. This means it would be a good substitute if you wanted a non-alcoholic Christmas cake that is rich and spicy. It is best left for at least 24 hours before serving to allow the flavors to develop and, if it can be resisted, it will continue to improve over succeeding days. This recipe allows for baking two cakes, one to eat and one to give away. If you only want one, halve the measurements!

- 1 cup / 240 ml honey
- 1 tsp cinnamon
- ½ tsp cloves
- ½ tsp nutmeg
- 1 cup / 150 g dark raisins
- ½ cup / 75 g currants
- ½ cup / 75 g chopped dates
- 1 cup / 115 g chopped walnuts
- 3 cups / 390 g cake/self-raising flour
- 2 tsp baking soda
- 1 tsp baking powder
- ¼ tsp salt
- ½ cup / 115 g butter, softened
- 1 cup / 250 g soft dark brown sugar, packed down to eliminate air pockets
- 4 large eggs, separated
- ¼ cup / 65 ml strong coffee

Heat the oven to 300°F/150°C/Gas Mark 3.
Grease and flour two 8-inch/20-cm x 4-inch/10-cm loaf pans.

1. In a small saucepan, mix the honey, cinnamon, cloves and nutmeg, and bring to a boil, mixing frequently. Remove from the heat and cool until it is lukewarm.
2. In a medium-sized bowl, combine the raisins, currants, dates and walnuts, and two tablespoons of the flour and mix well. Set aside.
3. In a separate bowl, mix together the remaining flour, baking soda, baking powder and salt. Set aside.
4. In a large bowl, beat the butter and brown sugar until creamy and smooth.
5. Add the egg yolks, one at a time, beating well after each addition.
6. Add the honey and mix well.
7. Add the flour and coffee alternately until well mixed.
8. Stir in the floured fruit and nuts. Set aside.
9. In a separate bowl, beat the egg whites until they are stiff and form peaks. Fold into the mixture, taking care not to over mix.
10. Divide the mixtures equally between the two loaf pans. Bake about for 60 minutes or until a skewer inserted in the middle of the cakes comes out clean.
11. Allow the cake/cakes to cool for about 20 minutes before removing to a wire rack so that they can cool completely.

INDEX